SIMPLE WAYS TO EDIT
DIGITAL PHOTOS

EASY-TO-USE TECHNIQUES FOR PICTURES WITH MAXIMUM IMPACT

How to use digital imaging tools to create perfect images,
with expert advice and 450 photographs and illustrations

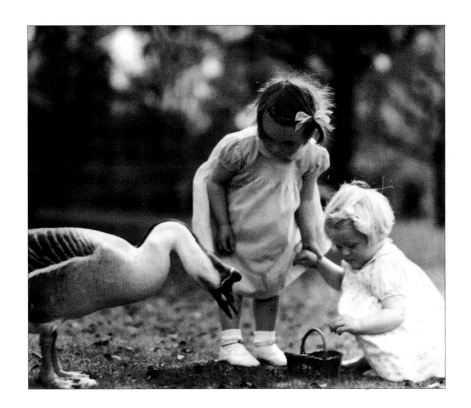

From adjusting contrast, cropping and cloning to making
cut-outs, using layers and creating montages • Steve Luck

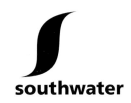

southwater

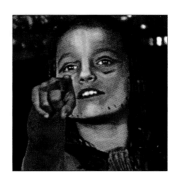
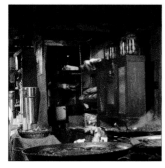
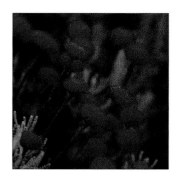
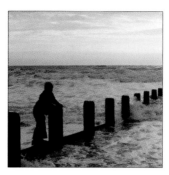

This edition is published by Southwater,
an imprint of Anness Publishing Ltd,
Blaby Road, Wigston, Leicestershire LE18 4SE

Email: info@anness.com

Web: www.southwaterbooks.com; www.annesspublishing.com

Anness Publishing has a new picture agency outlet for images
for publishing, promotions or advertising. Please visit our
website www.practicalpictures.com for more information.

Publisher: Joanna Lorenz
Project Editor: Elizabeth Young
Production Controller: Christine Ni

Designed and produced for Anness Publishing by
The Bridgewater Book Company Limited
Art Director: Lisa McCormick
Project Editor: Polita Caaveiro
Designer: Kevin Knight

ETHICAL TRADING POLICY

At Anness Publishing we believe that business should be
conducted in an ethical and ecologically sustainable way, with
respect for the environment and a proper regard to the
replacement of the natural resources we employ.

As a publisher, we use a lot of wood pulp to make high-quality
paper for printing, and that wood commonly comes from spruce
trees. We are therefore currently growing more than 750,000 trees
in three Scottish forest plantations: Berrymoss (130 hectares/320
acres), West Touxhill (125 hectares/305 acres) and Deveron Forest
(75 hectares/185 acres). The forests we manage contain more than
3.5 times the number of trees employed each year in making paper
for the books we manufacture.

Because of this ongoing ecological investment programme, you,
as our customer, can have the pleasure and reassurance of
knowing that a tree is being cultivated on your behalf to naturally
replace the materials used to make the book you are holding.

Our forestry programme is run in accordance with the UK
Woodland Assurance Scheme (UKWAS) and will be certified by the
internationally recognized Forest Stewardship Council (FSC). The
FSC is a non-government organization dedicated to promoting
responsible management of the world's forests. Certification
ensures forests are managed in an environmentally sustainable and
socially responsible way. For further information about this scheme,
go to www.annesspublishing.com/trees

PUBLISHER'S NOTE

Although the advice and information in this book are believed
to be accurate and true at the time of going to press, neither
the authors nor the publisher can accept any legal responsibility
or liability for any errors or omissions that may be made.

Previously published as part of a larger volume, *The Complete
Illustrated Encyclopedia of Digital Photography*

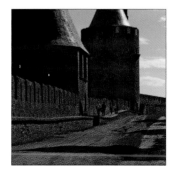
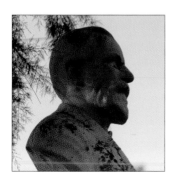
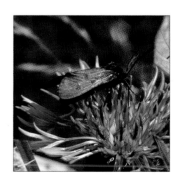
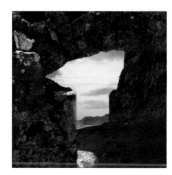

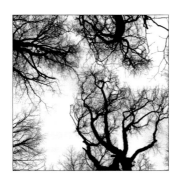
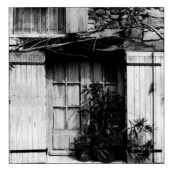
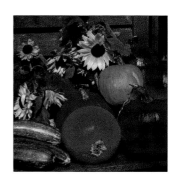
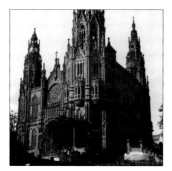

Contents

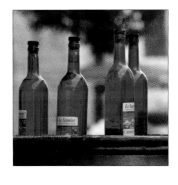
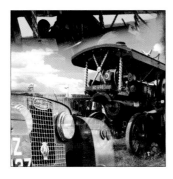
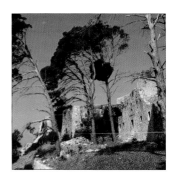
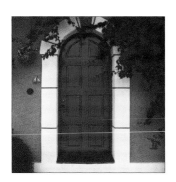

Introduction

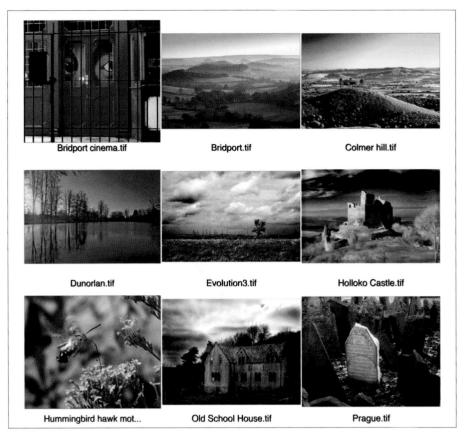

Bridport cinema.tif   Bridport.tif   Colmer hill.tif

Dunorlan.tif   Evolution3.tif   Holloko Castle.tif

Hummingbird hawk mot...   Old School House.tif   Prague.tif

With the advent of affordable, good-quality digital cameras and easy-to-use editing software for home computers, digital photography has become immensely popular.

A digital world

Being able to photograph everything and anything we want, pretty much with financial impunity, can be seen as a double-edged sword. On the one hand, it encourages experimentation – you only have to look at a website such as Flickr (www.flickr.com) to see some of the hugely creative things people achieve with their digital cameras, which are unlikely to have come about without the digital revolution. On the other hand, it also encourages a 'scatter-gun' approach to photography – keep firing and sooner or later you're

▼ Two separate images have been combined using some basic image editing software to create a fun photomontage.

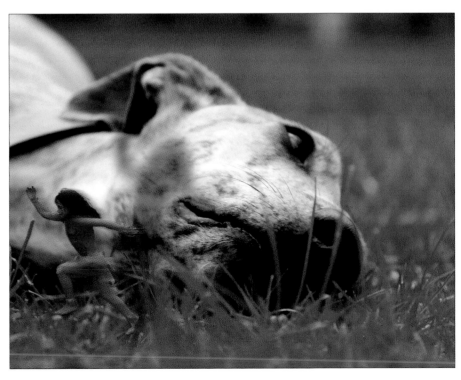

bound to come up with some good and interesting images. Although there's nothing inherently wrong with such an approach, it does in many ways negate the need or desire to learn. We need to slow down and look at our images in a more considered way – why does one shot 'work' when another from the same sequence fails? Why doesn't the image appear so full of movement? Why are the vibrant colours less intense? If we do this, we're going to increase our success rate, and by analysing what exactly it is about certain images that makes them stand out from the rest, we can mix the visual components a little to see what else works, and in that way our experimentation has some reason and method to it.

To be a good digital photographer it helps if you have a basic knowledge of how a digital image is created. Understanding the 'vocabulary' of digital imaging will make your learning curve much easier. It is also important to have a thorough knowledge of your equipment, particularly if you're either new to digital cameras or have 'upgraded' from a simple point-and-shoot to a more complex model. If you're reading this, then it's safe to assume that you have an appreciation for images and sights that you've seen and a desire to capture them in a way that most accurately reflects both how they appeared to you and what they meant to you.

◀ Contact sheets show a number of images on a single page. This is a great way to catalogue the images stored on a CD or DVD.

▶ A very good reason to keep a small library of different types of sky – stormy, cloudy or sunny – is that you never know when you'll want to superimpose a more interesting sky over a good shot with a dull sky; but be aware of the ethical compromise.

Editing techniques

As you gain proficiency and confidence with your photography it's likely that you'll want to assume greater control over your images once you've captured them.

This comprehensive book explains everything you'll need to know about using editing software to manipulate your photographs, from simple techniques such as darkening an image to more complicated tasks like enhancing skies for dramatic effect and retouching an old photograph.

The first chapter, Basic Image Editing, explains the basic concepts of how image-editing software works. It shows how to correct colour cast, crop, sharpen and clone images. This is followed by Advanced Image Editing, which introduces more complex techniques, from using layers and Photoshop filters to creating montages. They are by no means exhaustive, but should provide you with plenty of information to start experimenting and to see what these powerful applications can do.

The final chapter features a rundown of how to share your images – whether in colour prints or by using on-line libraries. There is also plenty of useful information on the different types of printers available, and how to produce the best prints at home. New products and services are springing up regularly, and here we show you just a few of the many ways in which you can share the images you've worked at and enjoyed creating.

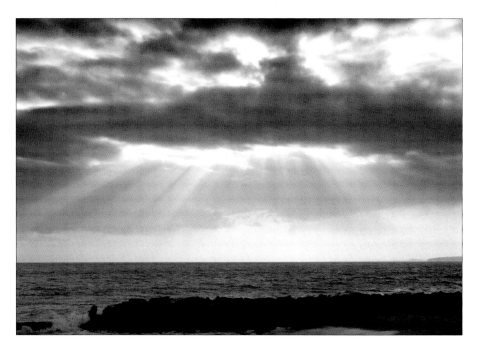

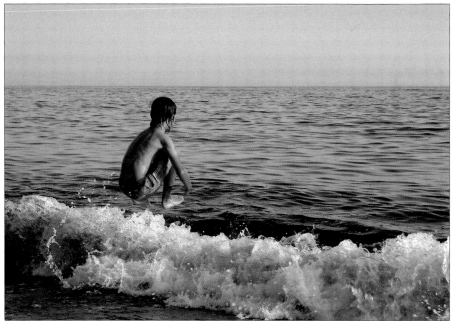

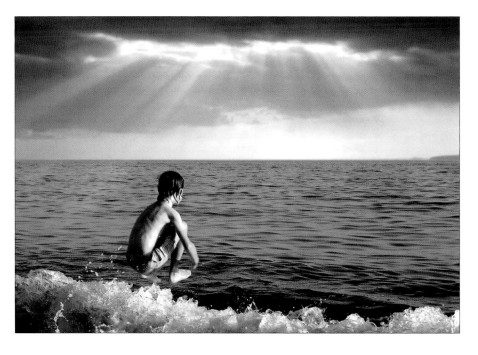

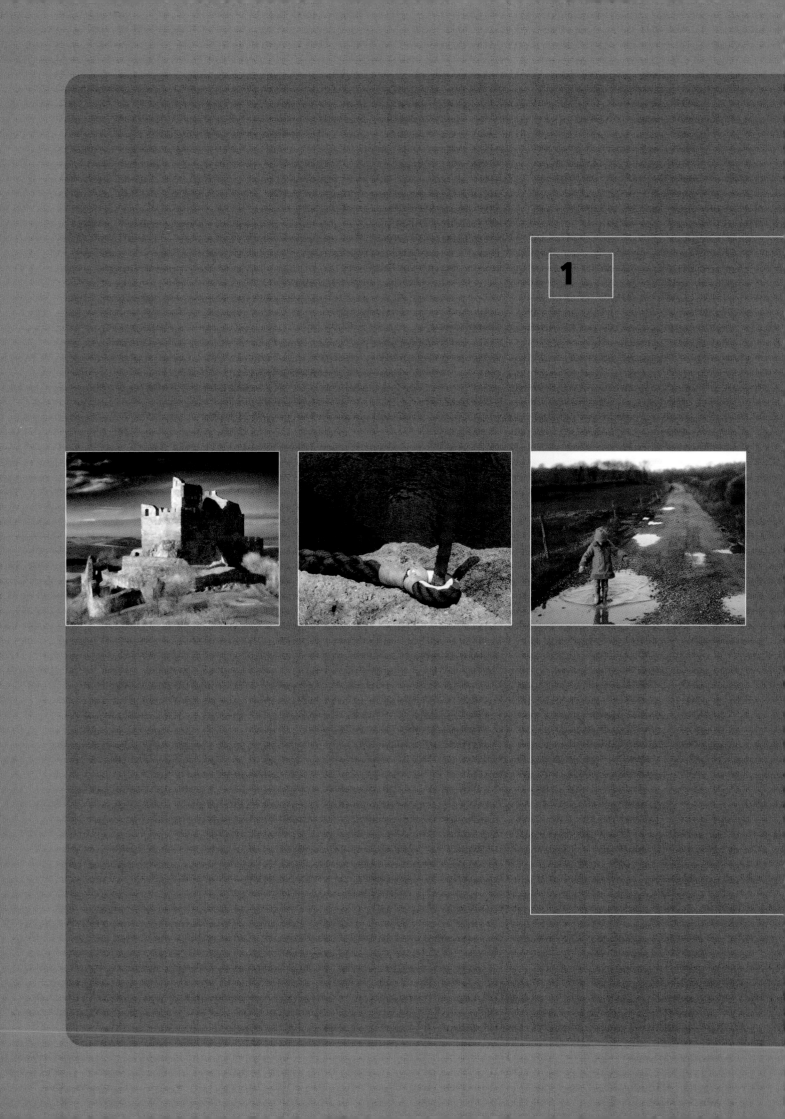

1

Basic Image Editing

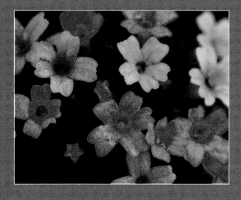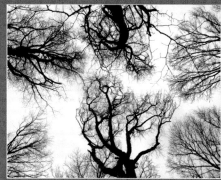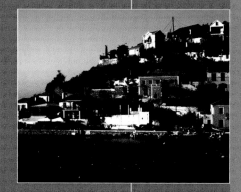

While most holiday snaps and family photographs can be printed
directly from the memory card or camera, for images you've really
worked on, and shot in RAW to maximize quality, you may want
control over the image's brightness levels, sharpness and so on.
This chapter looks at the basic image-editing tasks that help to
enhance your images. The projects are based either on Photoshop CS
(the industry-standard editing application) or Photoshop Elements
(the best-selling image-editing software), although other applications
– such as Corel's Paint Shop Pro or PhotoImpact – can perform
exactly the same tasks using very similar tools and menu commands.

Computers and Monitors

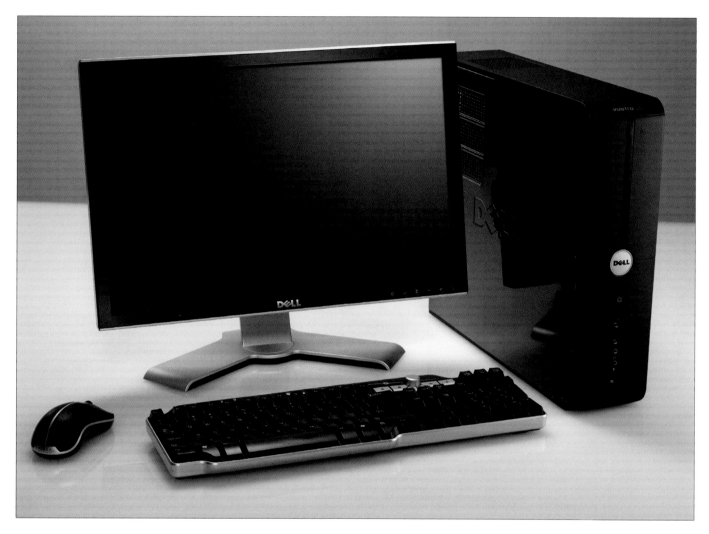

With computers being such a principal component of the modern digital photographer's workflow, it's worth spending a little time looking at the specifications and peripheral devices you'll find either necessary or useful for image editing and storing your digital photographs.

Processing specifications

Computer technology, along with digital camera technology, has come an extremely long way since the turn of the century. It is safe to say that just about any computer manufactured since around 2003 is likely to have sufficient processing power to run most image-editing software, but here are some specific details:

• If you work on a PC running Windows®, the minimum processing power you need is an Intel® Pentium® 4 or Intel Celeron® (or compatible) 1.3GHz processor, ideally with Windows XP or Vista and a minimum 512 megabytes (MB) of RAM (Random Access Memory). The absolute minimum hard disk space will be around 500MB, but most computers come with 80 gigabytes (GB) or more as standard, so this is rarely an issue.
• If you work on a Mac, make sure that it has a PowerPC® G3, G4 or G5 processor and that you're running OS X 10.3 or 10.4. Again, you may get away with running some software with 256MB of RAM, but the minimum is often 512MB.

ABOVE Choosing the right computer is important for image editing, as the software you need to run will place huge demands on its processor, memory, monitor and operating system.

For either operating system, the monitor should have a resolution of at least 1,024 x 768 pixels, with a 24-bit colour video card.

Your system should also have a built-in CD/DVD reader/writer so that you can load software and burn discs as a way of storing, sharing and backing up your images.

Finally, ensure that your computer system has appropriate connection ports; either USB, USB 2.0 or FireWire. These will enable you to download images directly from your camera or via a card reader, as well as provide connectivity for other peripherals, such as printers, scanners or external CD/DVD readers/writers.

With the computer specification detailed above you should be able to run most image-editing software, but remember that these are the minimum specifications and if you can afford to buy a computer with a higher spec, then do so.

Upgrading

If you find that your computer runs slowly, or that you can't use all the programs you'd like to use at one time, it may not be necessary to buy an entirely new system. There are numerous companies that produce memory upgrades that will be compatible with your computer and are relatively straightforward to install. A quick search on the Internet will usually provide a whole host of companies.

If you think your computer is running unreasonably slowly, you should check to ensure that you don't have any viruses, as these will affect your computer's performance. There are numerous examples of virus software available that can identify and remove most common viruses.

External hard drives

No matter how long you think the hard disk space on your new computer will last, sooner or later it will be filled with your digital pictures. Before you get to that stage, you may want to consider purchasing an external hard drive for extra space. External hard drives can also act as a backup for your images if, in the worst-case scenario, you experience a complete hard-drive failure.

Monitors

Your computer monitor is very important, as you'll be making adjustments to your images based on how accurately and consistently it displays tone and colour. Most modern monitors are more than adequate for image editing. All are capable of displaying the maximum 16.7 million colours, which is about the same number of colours distinguishable by the human eye. In addition, they also have a resolution of at least 1,024 x 768 pixels, which is perfectly adequate for just about all image-editing needs.

When choosing a monitor, the most important considerations are size and whether to have a CRT (Cathode Ray Tube) or an LCD (Liquid Crystal Display) screen. In terms of size, buy the biggest you can afford, as the larger the screen, the easier it is to display images at a good size, along with the various image-editing commands and dialog boxes. The drawback to a large monitor is the amount of room it takes up.

Historically, CRT screens provided brighter and richer colours, but modern LCD screens have become much better and are now perfectly capable of doing as good a job. Furthermore, flat LCD screens take up much less space.

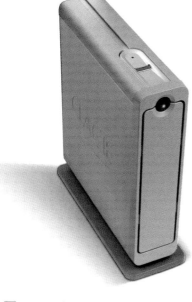

ABOVE When you start loading up your computer with digital photographs, the space on your hard drive will quickly fill up, irrespective of its size. An external hard drive that connects to your computer using FireWire or USB is the perfect answer.

BELOW FireWire and USB are the two most common ways of connecting peripheral devices to your computer. Some are very useful, such as printers and scanners, while others, such as a USB fan or torch, can be a bit more fun.

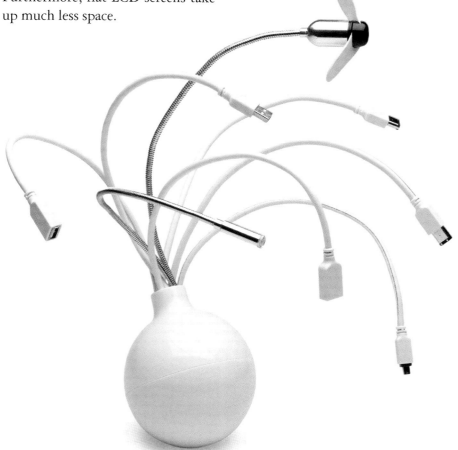

Image-editing Software

With digital photography now the principal method that most people use to capture their images, it's hardly surprising that there is a rapidly growing range of image-editing software available. The sophistication of image-editing software varies enormously, and this is reflected in the prices of the various packages – the most powerful, Photoshop, costs as much as a semi-professional dSLR. At the other end of the scale, there is software that you can download for free. Here's a quick rundown of the most popular examples.

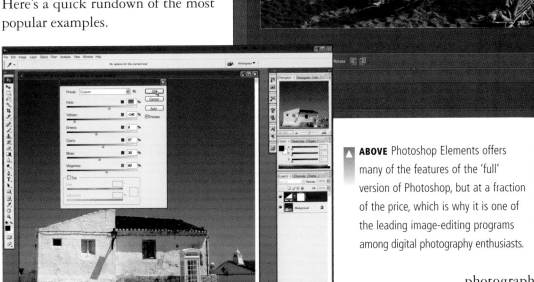

ABOVE Photoshop Elements offers many of the features of the 'full' version of Photoshop, but at a fraction of the price, which is why it is one of the leading image-editing programs among digital photography enthusiasts.

ABOVE The latest version of Adobe's powerful image-editing software, Photoshop, has a staggering array of editing commands and tools. One of the latest additions is the easy-to-use black and white conversion command.

Adobe Photoshop

For years the industry-leading image-editing software has been Photoshop, which is now in its tenth version and is available either separately as Photoshop CS4 or as part of Adobe's CS4 Creative Suite of applications. Although the most recent versions are likely to be prohibitively expensive for most amateur photographers, older versions can sometimes be found at a more affordable price and still offer a phenomenally powerful editing tool.

Adobe Photoshop Elements

Photoshop Elements is now in its ninth version for Windows and the Macintosh. Elements draws on its bigger brother for many of its features, including Layers and Blending Modes, as well as many of the more familiar commands, such as Levels, Sharpening, Hue/Saturation and so on. Few photographers would miss the features that don't appear in Elements. It is more geared to the photographer than Photoshop, and features Quick Fix editing tools specifically for digital images. Despite offering very powerful editing, viewing and sharing tools, Elements is an intuitive program and relatively easy to learn thanks to the layout, the program's structure and the various 'wizard', or help, functions.

Elements has also become an extremely capable image organizer. Images are automatically downloaded from the camera or card reader, then organized by date, and can be renamed by batch. Digital 'albums' can be created and filled by dragging and dropping images, while keywords are easily added to images, making them easier to find later on.

Corel Paint Shop Pro

Paint Shop Pro, also known as PaintShop Photo Pro X3. Similarly priced to Elements, Paint Shop Pro offers a very high degree of image-editing sophistication, with some features on a par with the full version of Photoshop. However, like Photoshop, getting to grips with Photo Pro X3 is a very steep learning curve, and in many ways less intuitive than Adobe's flagship application. There is a fair amount of help along the way, but the program is initially quite hard to grasp. But stick with it and Photo Pro X3 is a feature-rich software package that is capable of carrying out editing tasks to a high level.

Ulead PhotoImpact

Like Paint Shop Pro, PhotoImpact X3 provides good value for money for the features that it offers. The editing tools are powerful for such a low-cost application, and there are also a number of fun, if not strictly essential, filters.

Like Paint Shop Pro, however, PhotoImpact is not an instantly intuitive piece of software, and commands that should be readily accessible are not always easy to find. If you only want to make the most basic of changes to your images, and want software that easily organizes your images then PhotoImpact may not be the most appropriate package. But for more enthusiastic digital darkroom users, who are happy to spend a bit of time getting to know the software, PhotoImpact is a credible value-for-money alternative.

Serif PhotoPlus

Although now called PhotoPlus X4, the example we've included here is version 6, which is available as a free download. As such, it provides the basic editing functions, such as cropping, adjusting brightness and contrast, enhancing colour and removing red-eye. As a free piece of software, it offers the novice image editor a good introduction to basic image-editing tasks and is a good way to learn about image-editing workflow.

Unsurprisingly, those keen to stretch their creativity will quickly grow out of PhotoPlus and will be looking to other programs for more sophisticated functionality. The latest version includes layers and layer masks and, like Corel Ulead PhotoImpact, provides good value for money even if it does have a somewhat confusing user interface at times.

Free trials

There are several other basic image-editing programs available for free download on the Internet and your computer may come with one already installed. These programs tend to offer only the most basic features, but, if you're a complete novice, they can provide a good starting point. As your experience grows, you might want to upgrade to a more powerful program, and finding the one that is right for you depends on your specific needs. With so many software developers offering free trials, it's easy to take advantage of what's available and try out various packages for yourself.

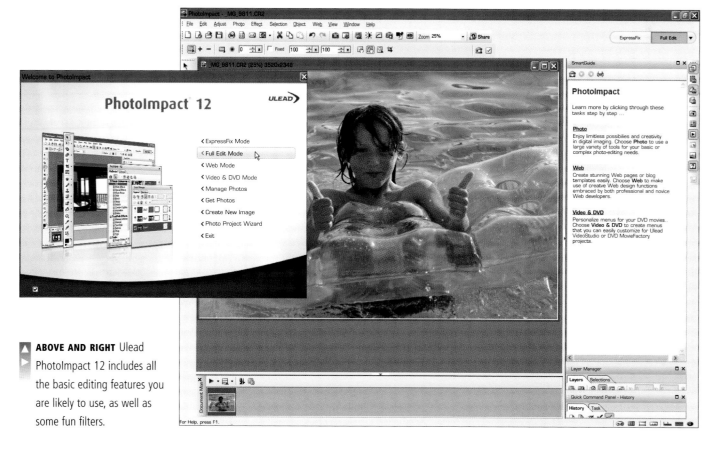

▲▷ **ABOVE AND RIGHT** Ulead PhotoImpact 12 includes all the basic editing features you are likely to use, as well as some fun filters.

Cropping and Rotating

As you take more photographs, framing your shots will become an instinctive part of the picture-taking process. As well as beginning to identify attractive compositions, you'll also find yourself starting to watch for vertical (or horizontal) edges to confirm that the camera is held level and that your images will turn out straight.

Sometimes, however, there just isn't time to worry about making sure everything's perfect, and it's all you can do to grab a shot at all before someone gets in the way. When a photograph comes out looking incorrectly aligned on your computer screen, the answer is to 'reframe' using image-editing software.

RE-FRAMING A PHOTO

This shot has a number of problems that could be tackled, but the key issues are cropping and rotation.

1 In Photoshop Elements, it's easy to straighten a shot using the Straighten tool, which you can find halfway down the main toolbox.

If you're using the full version of Photoshop this tool isn't provided, so skip to step 4 which will explain how you can rotate the image manually.

In the Options bar at the top, ensure the Canvas Options drop-down menu is set to 'Grow' or 'Shrink Canvas to Fit'. This means that your image will be left intact after it's straightened. To straighten the picture, click and drag along any line in the image that should be horizontal, such as the tops of the light grey front panels in the example shown here.

2 This seems to produce the correct result. If you want to check, go to View > Grid. Compare both the horizontal as well as the vertical features against the nearest gridlines. Unless the subject is shot straight-on, you may not be able to get everything perfectly straight, in which case it may be easier if you rotate the image manually, as explained in Step 4.

3 Once straightened, it is likely that you'll need to crop the photograph. You can crop any image that isn't composed as tightly as you'd like by selecting the Crop tool.

In the Options bar at the top, set Aspect Ratio to 'No Restriction', to crop freely.

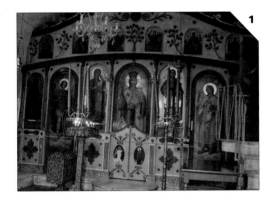
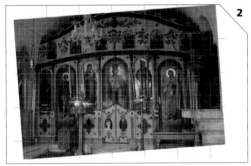
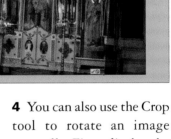
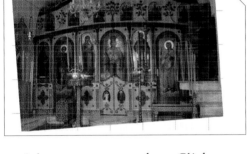

Click at one corner of the area you want to retain and drag diagonally to the other. The area outside is dimmed to indicate what will be cropped out of the picture. Drag any side or corner handle of the crop box to adjust it, then either click the green check symbol or press Enter to apply the crop.

This photograph has been cropped square to eliminate the blurred figures on the right. The midpoint of the altarpiece is aligned with the centre of the crop.

4 You can also use the Crop tool to rotate an image manually. First, display the grid (as in Step 2) before you activate and configure the Crop tool as in Step 3.

Drag around the rough area you want to crop to, then move the cursor just off any side or corner handle to show the rotation symbol. Click and drag to rotate the cropped area. Unfortunately, there's no option to display a grid that follows the rotated area, so you'll have to judge by eye.

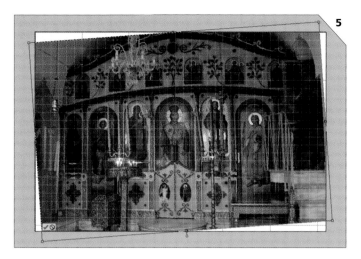
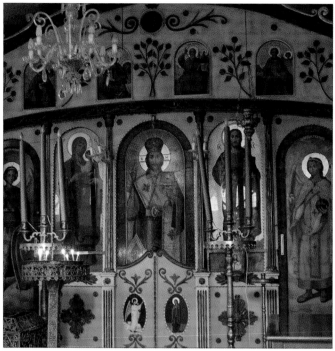

5 Alternatively, you can select the entire image by choosing Select > All, from the menu then Edit > Transform to reveal the Transform commands.

When you rotate the bounding box, the image rotates in real time, allowing you to check it against a grid.

However, the canvas isn't enlarged to accommodate the rotated image, so you may want to create some extra space. Use Image > Resize > Canvas Size and enter values that you think will be enough to encompass the rotated image. Unless you're rotating by a multiple of 90°, rotating is a fairly destructive process, so if you're at all unhappy with your first try, go to Edit > Undo to retrace your steps before rotating again. That way you'll retain as much of the image information as possible.

CROPPING TO A SPECIFIC SIZE

You can also crop an image by inputting the dimensions and resolution value in the Tool Options bar.

1 Here, we want to crop the image to 4in (10cm) square with a resolution of 300ppi.

2 Now you simply drag the Crop tool over the image. You can reposition the selection, if necessary, to ensure the best possible crop and click OK. The image will now automatically be 4in (10cm) square at 300ppi.

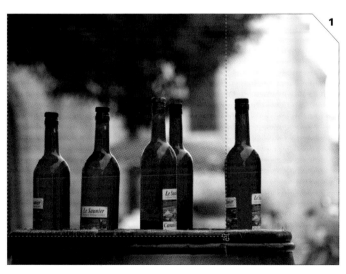

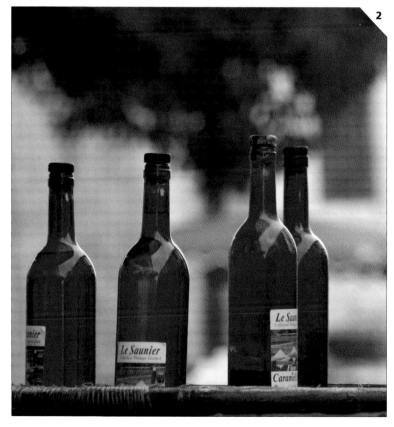

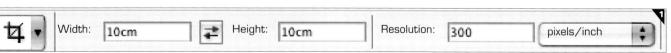

Brightness

Getting the exposure right every time isn't easy, no matter whether it's the photographer setting the controls or the camera's automatic function. Sometimes it just comes out wrong, and at other times there's a good excuse in the form of tricky lighting. The classic example is the situation where you have bright sunlight in the scene, but not on what you're shooting. Almost inevitably, while the shot's overall brightness may or may not be correct, your subject will look dull. When starting out with image-editing software, you may be tempted to reach for the Brightness command. Don't! It's rarely effective, and invariably destructive, discarding tonal information that can't be retrieved with further edits. Instead, turn to Levels, (here using Photoshop Elements) as explained in this project.

ADJUSTING BRIGHTNESS WITH LEVELS

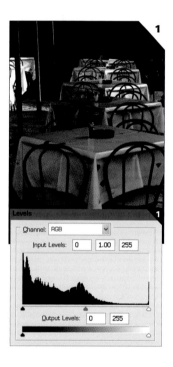

In this example, the image is slightly too dark.

1 Bring up the Levels dialog box by going to Image > Adjustment > Levels, where a histogram will show dark values at the chart's left, and light values at the right.

Here, pixel values are bunched at the dark end (left side) of the scale, with almost nothing brighter than a midtone except for a spike at the white end (right side), which represents the very few highlights in the image.

2 Two factors can make an image look dark; an absence of lighter values and the gamma (or grey) value. This is the location of the mid-point between white and black. To increase the gamma, click on the grey triangle below the histogram and drag it to the left.

If Preview is checked in the dialog box, the image will lighten. If pushed too far, increased gamma can make an image appear washed out so, in most instances, stop at about 1.4.

3 Now, to stretch the tonal range up into the lighter values, grab the white triangle at the right of the histogram and drag it to the left. Although it looks as if you're compressing the scale, you're actually expanding it. All those pixels represented by the black column above your marker become white, while the rest spread out across the scale, preserving the same relationships. The result is a brighter picture with more obvious light tones.

Bear in mind that any values to the right of your white marker will be 'burned out', which means they'll end up completely white, with highlight detail getting totally lost. Go too far and the image quality will suffer.

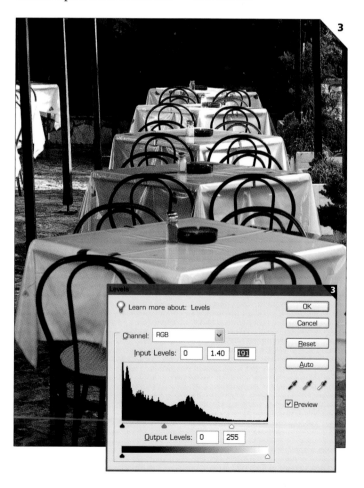

4 To see the effect you've had on the histogram, click OK when you're happy with how the picture now appears, then open the Levels dialog again via Image > Adjustment > Levels. The histogram shows a 'comb' pattern. Where tonal values are forced to spread out across the scale, gaps are left between them. This isn't a problem, but it represents a lack of tonal variation in the image and illustrates why an image that's shot right to start with will generally look richer than one you've had to correct using image-editing software.

5 There is another way to correct brightness by using the Levels dialog box. Making the assumption that your image is slightly too dark, click the white Eyedropper icon, situated at the right of the Levels dialog box. This gives you an Eyedropper cursor.

Move it onto the image and click on a point that's bright, but not the very brightest value in the image. The effect is similar to dragging the white marker on the histogram back to this value, with pixels of this brightness becoming white. Setting the white point also affects colour balance, so by clicking on a point that should be neutral or white you can correct a colour cast at the same time.

If a shot is too light, you can correct it by reversing the advice here – that is, by selecting the black Eyedropper icon and this time clicking on an almost black element of the image.

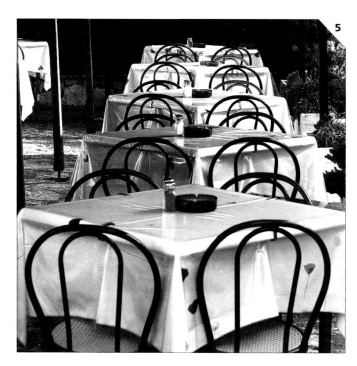

DARKENING AN IMAGE

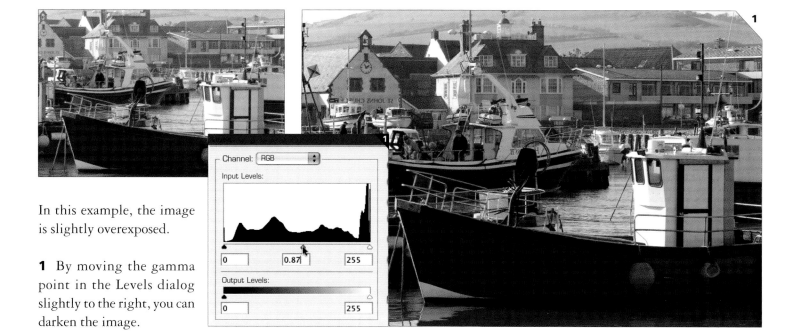

In this example, the image is slightly overexposed.

1 By moving the gamma point in the Levels dialog slightly to the right, you can darken the image.

Adjusting Contrast

There will be occasions when you've got the exposure right, but the picture still looks a little dull, and nine times out of ten the reason for this is a lack of contrast. While a lack of contrast can be a symptom of narrow tonal range, there's no hard-and-fast rule about how 'contrasty' a picture should be. It's really a matter of taste and what's appropriate for the specific image. For example, many classic monochrome landscape pictures have low contrast and rely on a subtle gradation of tone to maintain the viewer's attention. Most often though, you'll be looking to increase contrast to add impact to your pictures. Here's how to do it using Photoshop Elements.

INCREASING CONTRAST FOR IMPACT

Shot in hazy conditions, which hasn't been helped by the use of a telephoto lens, this image of cliffs has low-to-medium contrast.

1 To boost this contrast, go to Brightness/Contrast, which is found under Enhance > Adjust Lighting (in Photoshop Elements), or Image > Adjustments (in Photoshop). Increasing the Contrast setting to +40 gives a promising boost.

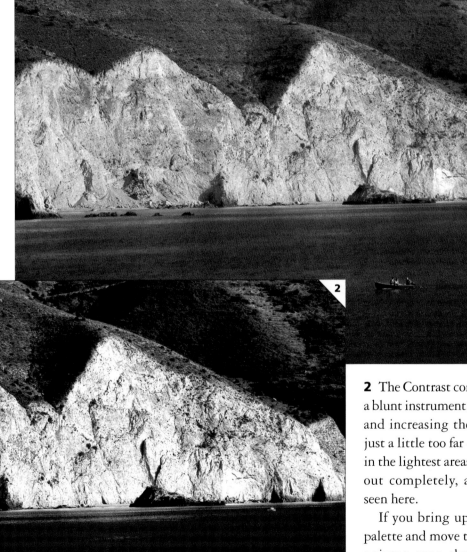

2 The Contrast command is a blunt instrument, however, and increasing the amount just a little too far can result in the lightest areas burning out completely, as can be seen here.

If you bring up the Info palette and move the mouse pointer over these areas, you'll see values of R=255, G=255, B=255 throughout, meaning that all the highlight detail is lost. This can happen even with modest adjustments.

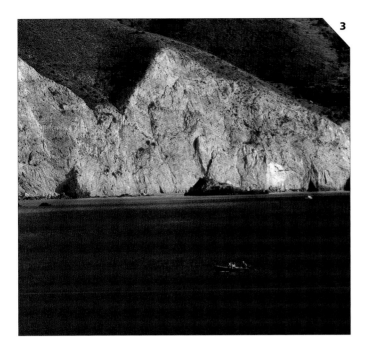

3 A far better option is to turn to the more powerful Levels command found under Image > Adjustments. In a low-contrast image, you will probably find that the histogram will show a lack of tonal values at the right and left ends of the scale – that is, the lightest and darkest values. Values cluster around the middle, falling off rapidly.

To correct this, grab the black and white markers in turn and drag them from the ends of the scale toward the middle. Leave each one at the point on the scale where the values start to rise. This gives a more subtle correction that leaves detail intact, allowing you then to control the result more precisely.

With some photographs, the histogram may appear to be all right, but the impression is still of low contrast. Moving the black and white points inward will still be effective, but make sure you watch out for lost detail in the shadows and the highlights.

4 Don't forget the gamma setting, represented by the grey marker in the middle of the histogram. Moving this to the left will emphasize the darker tones more, giving a bolder image. Moving it to the right will make the scene more pale and washed out.

Adjusting this setting along with the black and white points allows you to control the image's contrast and both the lightness and darkness independently. For example, here we've left the white marker alone, but have moved the black marker

well into the middle, then increased the gamma by dragging the grey marker toward it (that is, to the left). This gives the sea higher contrast and detail.

USING AUTO-CONTRAST

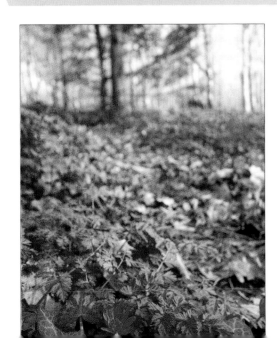
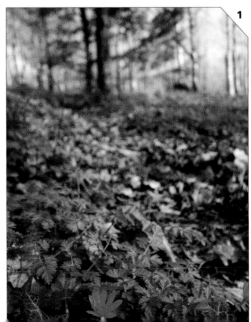

Here is another alternative to adjusting the black and white points manually in the Levels command.

1 Try Auto Contrast (found under Image > Adjustments > Auto Contrast). The effect is similar to performing Step 3 manually but this method has the added advantage of not affecting the colour balance as you can see here.

Correcting Colour Cast

Most digital cameras come with good Auto white balance (AWB) correction built in. This element of the camera's internal processing software analyses the scene you are shooting and attempts to correct any colour cast caused by strongly tinted light, such as that created by tungsten or fluorescent lighting. You can usually override the AWB correction and select the specific white balance mode that you want to use.

For example, if you are taking pictures indoors with incandescent lights or fluorescent striplights, you can select either of these options from the white balance menu and your camera will adjust the tone to be more natural, despite the ambient lighting conditions. However, these settings are seldom perfect and the camera can be tricked into making the wrong correction, which will result in a colour cast across the entire image.

USING LEVELS TO CORRECT COLOUR CAST

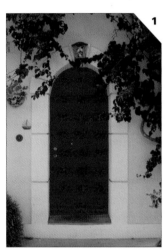

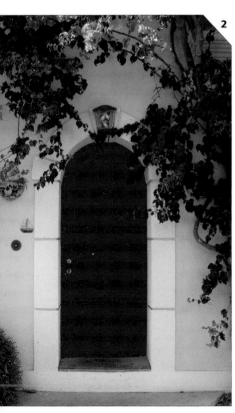

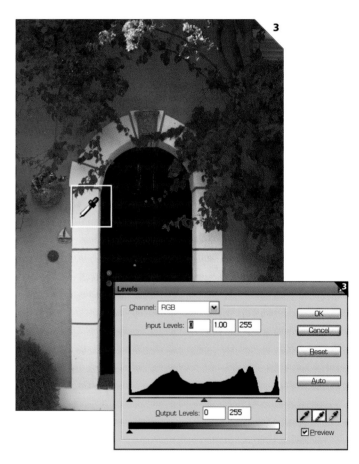

In the example shown here, the camera's Auto white balance was set to tungsten by accident, which has caused all sorts of colour issues.

1 A cold blue colour cast has affected the entire image, most obvious in the stone door frame, which should be brilliant white.

2 There are many methods you can use to correct colour cast problems in image-editing software, but by far the most powerful is the Levels command. Let's first try Auto Levels (Image > Adjustments > Auto Levels). When you are using Auto Levels, Elements finds the lightest and darkest pixels in each of the three colour channels (red, green and blue) and changes them to white and black respectively.

In this specific example, Elements hasn't done a very good job, and the resulting image has become too yellow and looks a little washed out. Use the Undo function (Edit > Undo) to revert to the previous image.

3 This time, let's see what happens when you take more control over the adjustment. Bring up the Levels dialog window, then click on the grey Eyedropper tool, which is the middle icon of the three found at the bottom right of the Levels dialog. Click on any grey part of the image with the tool, to tell Elements what the neutral tones are. Elements will rebalance the colours so that the area you clicked on becomes a neutral grey.

Don't be tempted to click on an area that is too bright or too white (such as the stone door frame), as this will give an entirely incorrect result, as shown in this example.

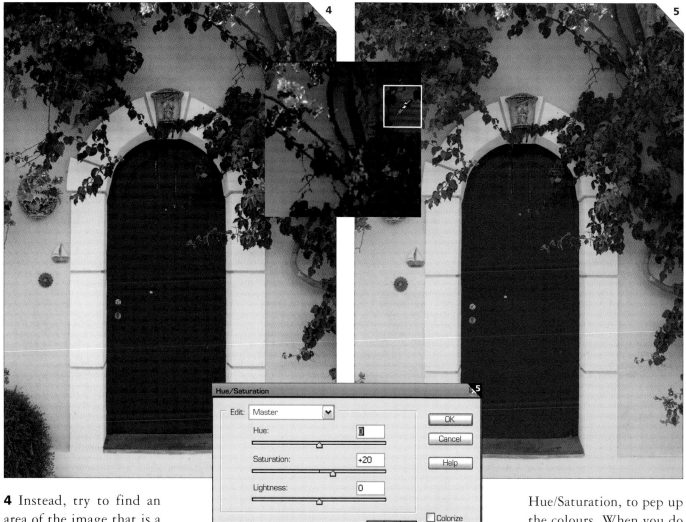

4 Instead, try to find an area of the image that is a midtone and which, had the image been correctly balanced to begin with, would have been close to a neutral grey. Here, a piece of stone cornice at the top right of the image has been selected. Clicking on the shaded areas in the grooves provides a much more accurate result.

5 Now the colour cast has been removed, it's often a good idea to increase the saturation using Enhance > Hue/Saturation, to pep up the colours. When you do this, you are safe in the knowledge that you won't be making the colour cast worse. Here, the saturation level has been increased by +20 to add more intensity to the colour.

USING AUTO COLOUR

Alternatively, you can try an automatic command to correct the orangey-yellow colour cast that is evident in this example.

1 The Auto Color command (which is found under Image > Adjustments > Auto Color) can sometimes be a bit hit and miss, but here it has successfully removed the colour cast of the street lamps in this outdoor café.

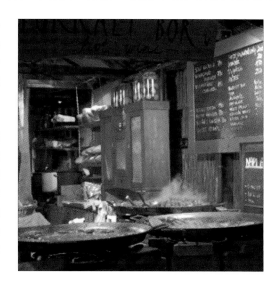

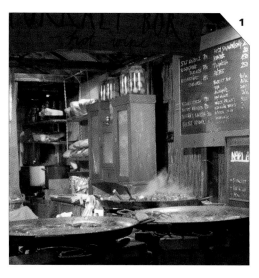

Curves

The Curves function is one of the tonal adjustments that is most often used by professional retouchers. The progression from dark to light in the image is depicted as a diagonal line, which you can reshape into a curve – or whatever shape you wish – to render the picture's tone exactly as you want it. Curves is a long-standing key feature of Photoshop, enhanced in recent versions to offer more information and control over individual colour channels. It has also been recently introduced into Photoshop Elements.

ADJUSTING TONE WITH THE CURVES TOOL

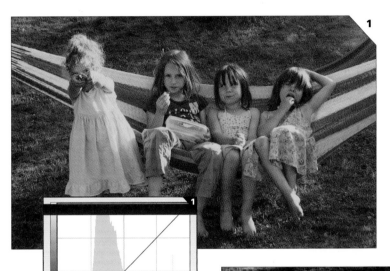

1 An extremely powerful and versatile tool, Curves can be used to adjust the tone of any photograph, but it's also a useful alternative to Levels for boosting a shot that looks a little flat and dull, such as this one.

Start by going to Image > Adjustments > Curves to open the Curves dialog box. As with Levels, you're shown a histogram in which each vertical bar represents the number of pixels of a certain value, from dark at the left of the scale to light on the far right. Overlaid on this histogram is a diagonal line that shows the relationship between the original image (or 'input') on the horizontal axis, and the result of the Curves function (or the 'output') on the vertical axis.

2 With this particular image, the grey histogram in the background (shown in Photoshop CS3) fades off at both ends of the scale, indicating there is a lack of shadows and highlights.

As with Levels, you can shift the black and white points to fix this by dragging the markers at the left and right of the horizontal axis toward the middle. Move them to where the values start to climb and you'll see the end points of the diagonal line will then move along with them.

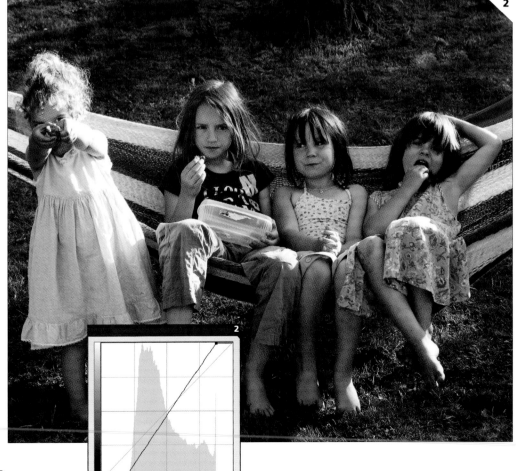

3 In the Levels dialog, you could then adjust the overall tone by moving the central grey or gamma slider to the left or right. Curves gives you greater control of the progression from dark to light. Click on the middle of the diagonal line and drag downward. The picture will look darker overall as shadows become deeper, but it still retains the brightness and detail of the highlights.

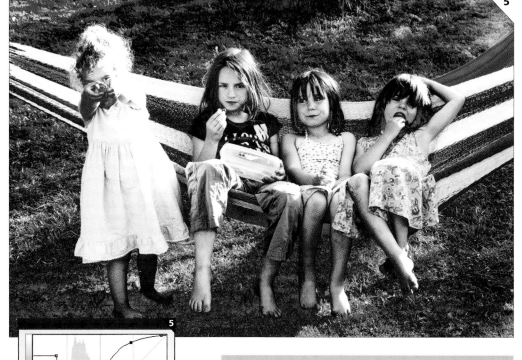

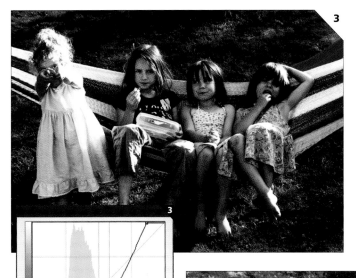

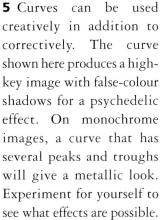

4 To brighten things up, click near the top right of the curve to add a second point. Drag this point upward and the curve will change shape. You now have what is commonly known as an 'S-curve'. Darkening the shadows and lightening the highlights in this way will create a bold, high-contrast image.

5 Curves can be used creatively in addition to correctively. The curve shown here produces a high-key image with false-colour shadows for a psychedelic effect. On monochrome images, a curve that has several peaks and troughs will give a metallic look. Experiment for yourself to see what effects are possible.

In general, when you're not aiming for special effects, your curve should remain smooth and, from left to right, each point should be higher than the last. Otherwise you'll create areas of flat, featureless colour within the image.

Unless you need to bring in the white and black points, make the curve continue smoothly to each end of the scale, without flattening out. This avoids the problem of clipping shadows or highlights.

Preserving colours

Notice how colour, as well as lightness, is affected as you adjust the curve. As the image gains contrast, colours also become more saturated. If you want to adjust contrast while preserving colours, switch your image from RGB to Lab mode (Image > Mode > Lab color) before using the Curves command. You can then adjust the curve for the Lightness channel only, which affects contrast and not colour.

Dodging and Burning

The slightly strange-sounding terms of 'dodging' and 'burning' hark back to the days of the traditional darkroom. Both terms refer to localized print-exposure control as the photosensitive photographic paper is exposed to the light from the film enlarger.

For example, a common use of burning is to ensure a bright sky is sufficiently exposed to bring out detail in the clouds. The photographer will make a rough mask of the foreground, and, after a set time, use the mask to cover the foreground so that the sky receives a few more seconds of exposure to the light, therefore making it darker. Dodging works in the opposite way. If parts of the image are in deep shadow, the photographer will make a mask to cover those areas part way through the print-exposure time. By doing this, he or she reduces the light striking the shadow areas, making them lighter than the rest of the image so that they hold fine shadow detail.

The digital versions of dodging and burning tools are intended to replicate these effects. In other words, they allow specific parts of an image to be made either lighter or darker, primarily to bring out detail in those regions that might otherwise be lost.

ADJUSTING LIGHT AND SHADOW

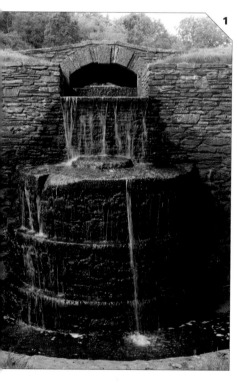

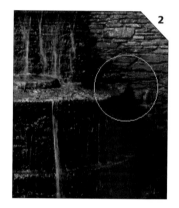

1 This photograph of a water feature was taken on an overcast day. Detail has filled in the darkest (under-exposed) regions of the photograph, while the top of the feature and the trees beyond are overexposed and have taken on a faded look. With careful dodging and burning, we should be able to balance the two regions.

2 To extract the detail from the darkest shadows, select the Dodge tool from the Toolbox. Make sure that the Exposure is set to between 5% and 10% in the Tool Options bar, and then set the Dodge tool to Shadows, using the drop-down menu in the Tool Options bar. Now adjust the tool to an appropriate size and then 'paint' over the worst offending areas.

You might discover that the results are sometimes a bit slow to appear, and rather than lightening the area, the Dodge tool can sometimes make the area appear a little cloudy.

3 To darken any over-exposed areas, select the Burn tool (it's in the same location as the Dodge tool), but this time use an Exposure setting of around 50% and select Midtones from the Tool Options bar. Brush the Burn tool over any overexposed areas. The Burn tool does a better job of darkening highlights than the Dodge tool does of lightening shadows, but control is still quite tricky.

4 Because the Dodge and Burn tools are tricky to control, the most effective way to dodge and burn areas of an image does not involve using these tools.

Instead, begin by creating a new blank layer by clicking on the 'Create a new layer' icon at the top of the Layers palette. In the Blending Modes menu at the top of the Layers palette, change the Blending Mode to Overlay.

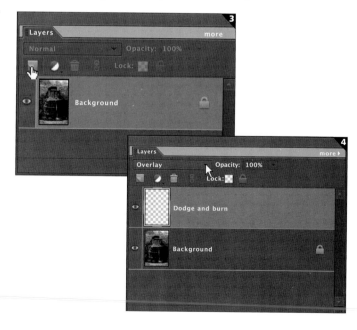

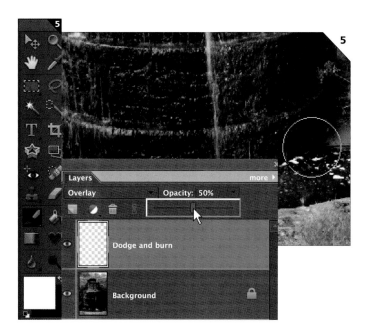

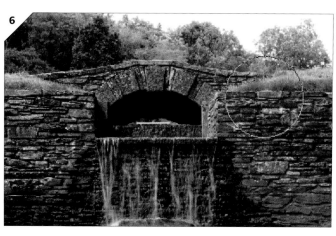

5 Select the Brush tool in the Toolbox, and click on the default Background/ Foreground icon at the bottom of the Toolbar to ensure that the Foreground and Background colours are black and white.

Next, click on the small right-angle arrow icon next to the default colour icon to exchange them, so that white is now the foreground colour. Use the square bracket keys to set an appropriate brush size, and in the Tool Options bar set the Opacity to a value between 30% and 50%. As before, paint over the shadow areas. You should notice that the adjustment is much quicker than before and that the lightening effect is much more successful than using the Dodge tool.

You can also increase or decrease the Opacity if you want to increase or decrease the dodging effect. Another option is to increase or decrease the layer's Opacity in the Layers palette.

6 To replicate the Burn tool, you simply select black as the foreground colour. As previously, paint over the overexposed highlights to darken them and add some colour. Notice how the trees and foreground grass now look much more vibrant. Again, you can use the Opacity slider in the Tool Options bar if you want to adjust the strength of the burning effect.

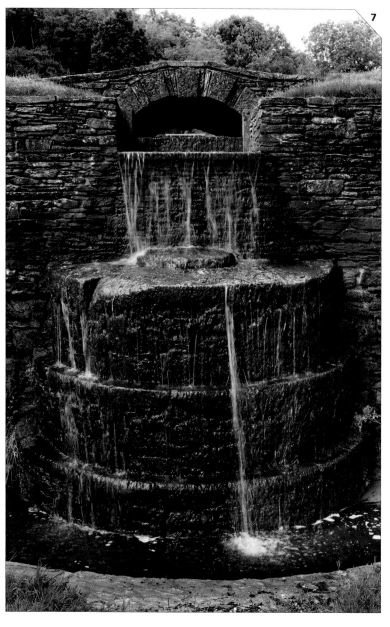

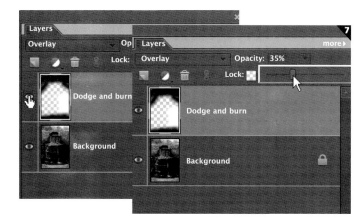

7 When you're happy with the overall adjustment, try clicking on the Dodge and Burn layer's visibility eye to turn it off and on.

This shows an instant 'before and after' of the effect that the layer is having.

If you wish, you can go back and paint black on any over-dodged areas and vice versa. Alternatively, you have the option of reducing the overall Opacity of the Dodge and Burn layer as well, to reduce the intensity.

Sharpening

Sharpening is one of the most important functions of image-editing software. Although used primarily when images have been shot using the RAW files format, (which therefore require some post-production editing), sharpening can also help when you find a shot isn't perfectly focused, just as long as the problem isn't too severe. Even on pictures that already look crisp, an additional amount of sharpening can ensure detail really pops out, especially if you are going to make a print. Sharpening also has an important technical function in countering the softening caused by scaling an image to make it larger or smaller.

APPLYING UNSHARP MASK

1 Before you think about sharpening any image, it is best to view it at 100% magnification first – that is, with one pixel on the screen representing one pixel in the image. For corrections such as tone and colour adjustments, you'd want to zoom out so that you can see the whole image, but sharpening can only be judged at 100%.

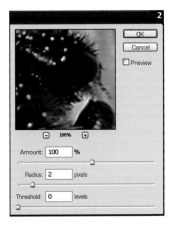

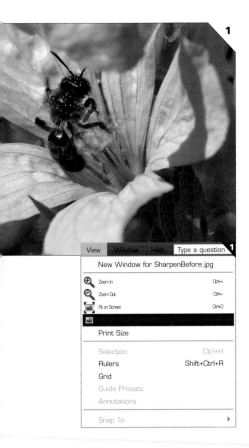

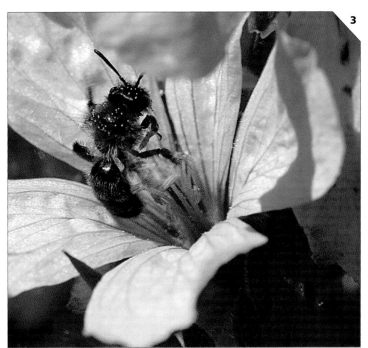

2 The best command to use for almost all sharpening purposes is Unsharp Mask. The name reflects the fact that this filter works by subtracting a blurred copy of the image. It's a digital version of a technique which is used in traditional image processing. In all versions of Photoshop, the command is found in Filter > Sharpen. However, in Photoshop Elements 5, it was moved to the Enhance menu.

Choosing Unsharp Mask brings up a dialog box that contains three sliders and a small preview window. Tick the Preview box to see the result on the main image, or untick it to compare the preview against the original. Your task is to find the right slider settings for your picture. Start by trying Amount: 100%, Radius: 2, Threshold: 0. With low-resolution images, use a Radius of 1 for greater sharpening.

3 See what effect this has on the image. Most images will have limited depth of field, so concentrate on the areas that are meant to be in focus. It's these that you're aiming to sharpen.

The bee in this high-resolution picture needs to be sharp, to draw the eye and create contrast with the softer petals, giving us an

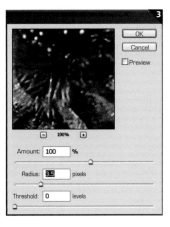

impression of the world at the insect's scale. To do this, increase the Radius setting until the detail becomes noticeably harder-edged. Here, 3.5 pixels is enough.

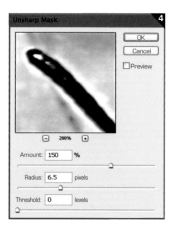

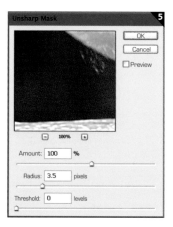

4 You can also increase the Amount if you need to create a stronger effect. It's important not to increase these settings too far though, so watch out for 'halos' around edges and a loss of subtle detail.

In this case, slightly over-zealous sharpening has created a marked glow around the bee's antenna, whereas the highlight detail has filled in.

5 Having set the first two sliders for the best result on key areas of detail, use the third, the Threshold slider, to mitigate any unwanted side effects.

Here, the low-contrast background areas, such as the distant foliage behind the petals, originally looked smooth, but the Unsharp Mask brings out noise (digital grain) in smooth areas of the image.

Sharpening down

When you print an image using a four-colour process (which is the method used to produce this book), the pixels are converted into dots of ink using half-toning. This has a softening effect, so to keep the picture looking crisp, you should sharpen a little more than normal. The dithering, or stochastic screening, method used in modern inkjet printing has less effect on sharpness.

It's often said that a digital image cannot be enlarged beyond its proper size without loss of quality, but it can safely be reduced. That's not strictly true, because when an image is reduced in size, it won't appear nearly as sharp. Before printing a high-resolution photograph at a small size, resample it using Image > Resize > Image Size. At the bottom of the dialog box, tick Resample Image and set the resampling method to Bicubic Sharper. Then enter the required physical dimensions under Document Size and click OK.

For even better results, especially with very small printed images, try resampling in stages, reducing by no more than 70% each time, using Bicubic Sharper. Apply Unsharp Mask at 100% with a 0.5 pixel Radius to the final, reduced image.

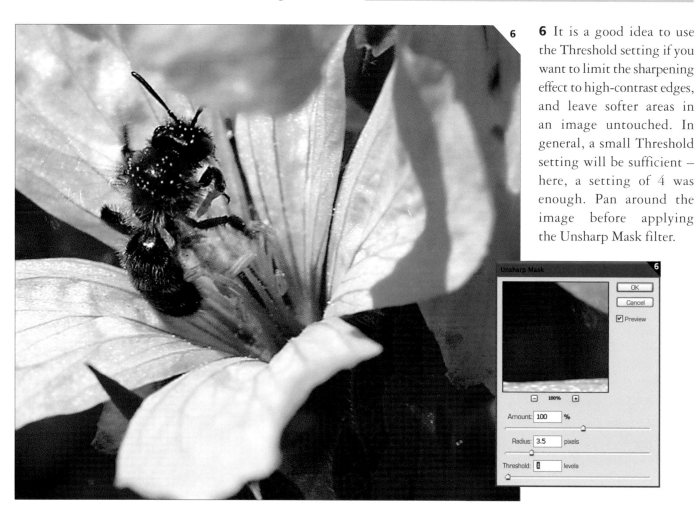

6 It is a good idea to use the Threshold setting if you want to limit the sharpening effect to high-contrast edges, and leave softer areas in an image untouched. In general, a small Threshold setting will be sufficient – here, a setting of 4 was enough. Pan around the image before applying the Unsharp Mask filter.

Advanced Sharpening

Some photographs present a challenge because they're substantially out of focus. This may be due to slightly inaccurate manual focusing, a subject being in motion at the time the picture was taken, the camera's autofocus picking out the wrong part of the scene or autofocus being compromised by low light.

Software sharpening can never completely correct poor focus, but it can help to restore a reasonable impression of sharpness. However, it is very difficult to achieve this without serious unwanted effects. Limiting unwanted effects requires more advanced techniques than simply applying the Unsharp Mask, as shown here.

MANUALLY IMPROVING FOCUS WITH UNSHARP MASK

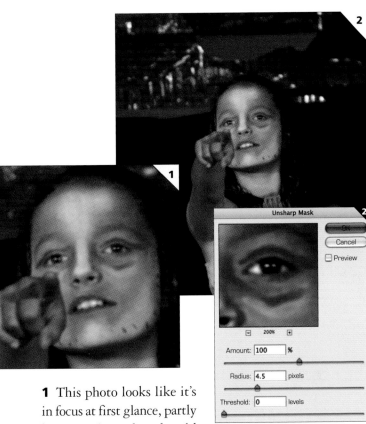

1 This photo looks like it's in focus at first glance, partly because the red and gold decoration in the background is unfocused, which makes the foreground subject look sharp by comparison.

At 100%, however, you can see that the face is very soft, with the eyes in particular lacking the hard detail that would give the shot real impact.

On your own photograph, identify an area such as this where you feel you need to concentrate your efforts.

2 It may be helpful to zoom to 200% in order to get a really clear view, then go to Filter > Sharpen > Unsharp Mask and set the sliders to a base level, as discussed earlier. On such a soft image, there'll be little or no visible improvement, so increase the Radius until you start to get an actual result. In the image shown here, there's a noticeable boost at 4.5 pixels.

3 Such strong sharpening produces side-effects you don't really want, such as distinct halos around edges and an increase in noise. Part of the reason for this is that you're working on a colour image, and increasing the contrast at the edges also has an impact on the appearance of the colours. To avoid this, you just need to separate the light and dark tone information from the colour information. This can be easily done by simply switching your image from the normal RGB colour mode, where three channels store the red, green and blue values for each pixel, to Lab Colour.

To change to Lab Colour, cancel the Unsharp Mask dialog box and select Image > Mode > Lab Color.

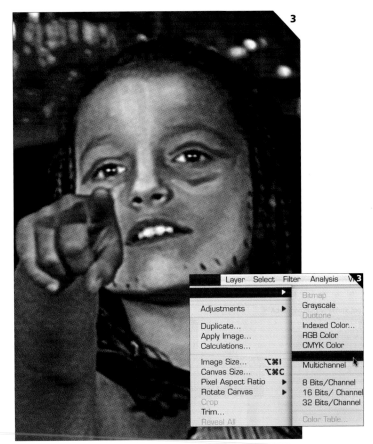

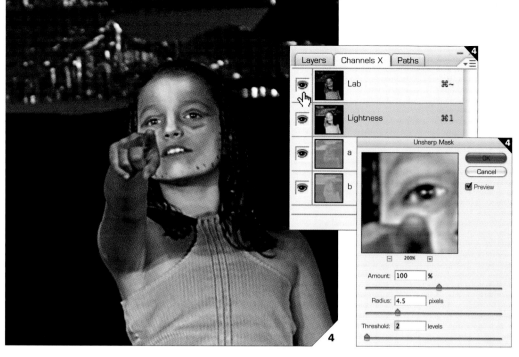

4 If you look at the Channels palette, you will see the image is stored as 'a' and 'b' channels (which contain colour information), plus Lightness.

Click the Lightness channel and the image then appears in monochrome, showing only the lightness of each pixel, rather than its colour. Click the box to the left of the composite Lab channel at the top to re-display the 'Eye' icon. Although you're viewing the full colour image, you will only be working on the Lightness channel when you apply the sharpening.

Open the Unsharp Mask filter and you'll see the preview within the dialog box reflects the monochrome Lightness channel. You should now find it easier to set a Radius that gives a clear improvement, but without excessive halos.

Watch for excessive noise in the low-contrast areas, but a small Threshold, such as 2 pixels, should be more than sufficient to fix this in most cases.

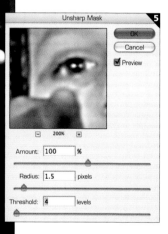

5 Using higher settings isn't the only way in which you can increase the effect of sharpening. It can be more effective to sharpen twice, so go back to Unsharp Mask and try a smaller Radius, and, if necessary, use a higher Threshold to avoid noise.

Smart sharpen

Adobe offers another sharpening command that has the option of using a method similar to Lab conversion to minimize unwanted effects, while keeping your image in RGB. If in Photoshop, go to Filter > Sharpen > Smart Sharpen. If you're using Photoshop Elements 5, then go to Enhance > Adjust Sharpness.

The Remove drop-down menu provides a selection of methods. It's possible to minimize halos by selecting Lens Blur, but you'll probably discover that you need stronger settings to get a visible improvement. There's no Threshold control here, so you don't have direct control over any resulting noise.

In Photoshop, you can click Advanced for extra controls that limit the sharpening effect to shadow or highlight areas. This can be a very useful feature if the sharpening settings that give the best result in the area of interest cause excessive halos or noise in other areas.

One way to think of it is that the first Unsharp Mask brings out edges from the background, and the second Unsharp Mask sharpens those edges. When you've got the best result, convert the image back to RGB using Image > Mode > RGB Color.

Cloning Tools

Cloning tools are an important feature of most image-editing programs. They are powerful editing tools that in simple terms copy, or 'clone', the pixels from one area of an image and place them over another part of the image. This is usually done in order to remove unwanted marks, blemishes or even entire objects. Because there is a number of different types of elements that you might occasionally want to remove, most image-editing software packages offer a range of cloning tools. These make it easier to ensure any corrections that you make are all but invisible to see, and they speed up the image-editing process. Here we'll look at the main Cloning tools offered by Photoshop, but other applications offer a range of very similar tools.

Spot Healing Brush

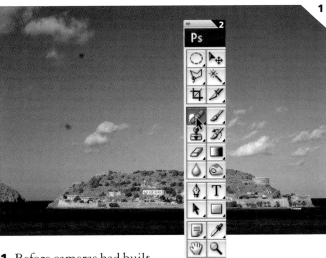

1 Before cameras had built-in dust removal systems, dSLR users would suffer from dust entering the camera body and attaching itself to the image sensor.

Even with these new dust removal systems, dust can still find its way onto the sensor. It manifests itself as dark spots that are most noticeable in uniformly coloured areas of an image, such as a very clear blue sky. They also become far more obvious when a small aperture is used.

The spots will continue to appear in the same place, frame after frame, until the sensor is cleaned.

2 Both Photoshop and Photoshop Elements have the perfect tool for deleting dust spots from images; the Spot Healing Brush.

Simply select the tool from the Toolbox and adjust the brush size using the '[' and ']' keys until the brush cursor fits neatly over the offending spot. Then all you need to do is click the mouse button.

3 The same tool works equally well on any skin blemishes, such as spots, freckles and moles.

The Spot Healing Brush has two options available in the Tool Options bar. Proximity Match samples pixels from around the edge of the selection to replace the blemish, while Create Texture samples all the pixels in the selection.

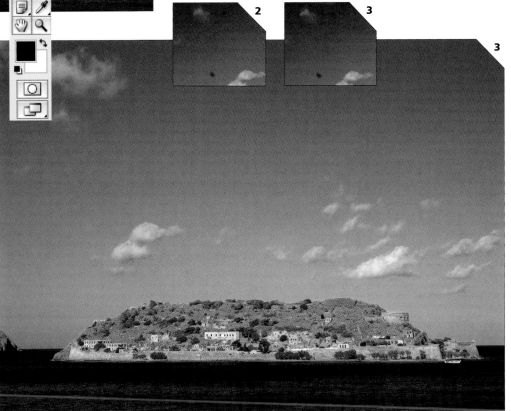

Healing Brush

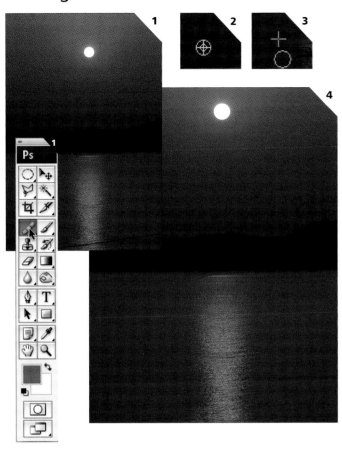

1 The Healing Brush tool is twinned with the Spot Healing Brush and works in a similar way. The sunset image shown here suffers from having a telegraph cable running along the bottom edge, which was unavoidable.

2 Select the Healing Brush from the Toolbox and use the '[' and ']' keys to adjust the brush size. The tool works more effectively if you use a soft brush.

To begin sampling, hold down the Alt key as close as you can to the start of the area that you want to replace. The Round Brush icon will then turn into a target to indicate that the tool is now in 'sample' mode. This signals that you can now begin to fix the problem area, in this case, the telegraph cable.

3 Sample the area and then paint over the offending cable. You'll notice a cross near to the brush symbol, which moves along as you paint. This indicates the area that the tool is sampling. Here, for example, the tool is automatically sampling from the golden coloured water as it moves along the cable.

4 Removing the cable from this photograph took a matter of seconds using the Healing tool.

Clone Stamp

1 If the area that you want to replace is comparatively large and the region from which you are sampling is not a uniform pattern, the best tool to use is the Clone Stamp tool. In this image, for example, it would look better if the large sign on the rocks could be removed.

2 As with the Healing Brush, start by selecting an appropriately sized soft brush and then hold down the Alt key to sample the part of the rock that you want to copy.

3 When you've done this, release the Alt key and then click with the brush on the area that you want to replace. You may find that clicking the brush more than once helps to delete the area.

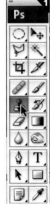
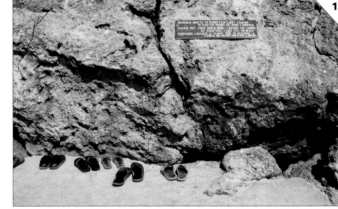
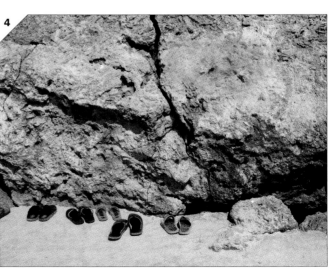

4 Continue to sample from different regions to avoid creating regular patterns of tell-tale signs of cloning. You may find that you need to go over parts of the image that have already been sampled. By adjusting the brush size and sampling from various parts of the image, you should soon be able to create a realistic-looking replacement area of rock face.

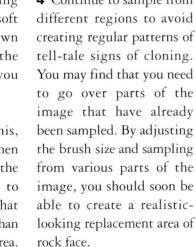
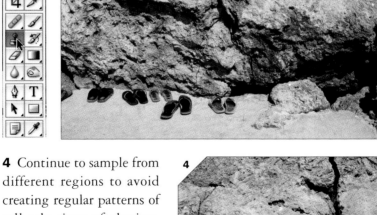

Advanced Cloning

The Clone tool is an indispensable item in Photoshop's and Photoshop Elements' tool chests. If you have unwanted objects or artefacts in your image that spoil an otherwise perfect shot, the Clone tool is probably the first tool to reach for. By allowing you to sample and paint using nearby pixels, you can use this tool to effectively eradicate, extend or duplicate elements in your scene – usually with a few strokes of the mouse.

DISCARDING UNWANTED ELEMENTS

1 In this photograph, modernity is encroaching on an otherwise picturesque, rooftop townscape. You could probably get away with leaving in the aerials, but the satellite dishes have to go. Here, the Clone tool comes to the rescue.

2 Start with the removal of the satellite dish on the right. First, begin by sampling an area of stone wall from anywhere around the dish by holding Alt and clicking on the image. Don't click too close, but not too far either, from the area you want to remove from the picture.

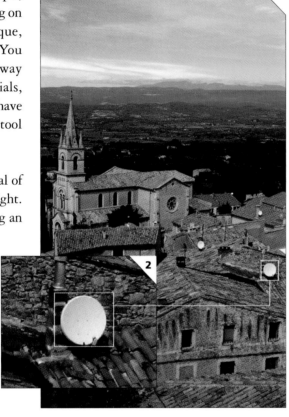

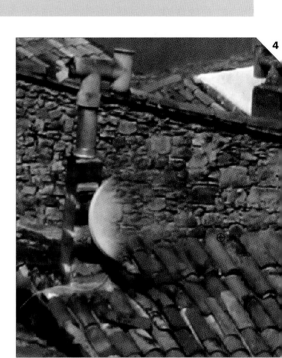

4 To replicate the top edge of the roof tiles, place the Clone tool over an existing edge section, and clone out the appropriate part of the dish. You may find using a harder brush provides a cleaner, more distinct line.

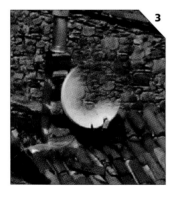

3 Set the Clone tool's brush to a smallish size, sample the wall and, using single clicks, cut out the part of the dish that's in front of the wall.

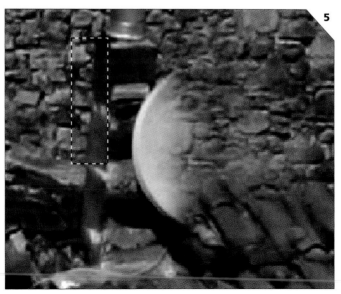

5 For areas that contain straight lines and in which there is a great deal of contrast between one region and the neighbouring one, such as the edge of the chimney stack 'overlapping' the stone wall in the background, the best method is to draw a selection around the existing side and copy it. Now we'll paste the copied selection over the remaining part of the satellite dish.

6 After roughly positioning the copied selection, use the transform commands to flip the section and rotate it into the right position. Flatten the layers and tidy up the new section using the Clone tool as before.

7 You can do the same with the remaining smaller dishes, cloning them out carefully, but always paying close attention to what patterns of pixels are immediately around them. If you choose your sample areas carefully, the final result should be a seamless image free from any unsightly satellite dishes.

When undertaking detailed cloning work such as that shown here, it pays to zoom right in when doing the cloning and then zoom out to normal size to see the correction in context.

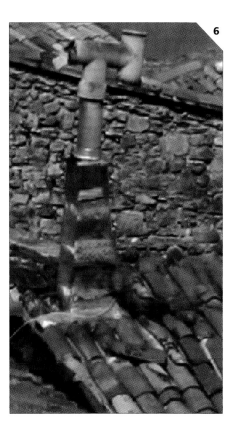

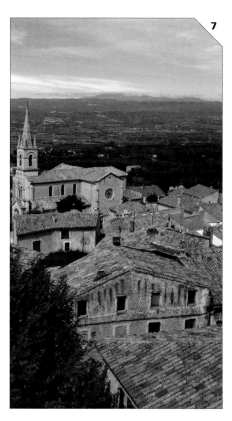

REMOVING AN IMAGE WITH THE PATCH TOOL

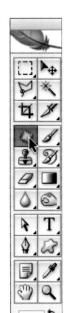

Photoshop also has a powerful, quick and easy tool for removing just about any item, from small facial blemishes to entire objects. It's called the Patch tool.

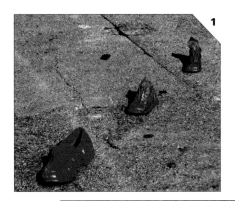

3 Once you have made the selection, click and drag it to an area on the image that most closely resembles the background of the object that you are trying to remove, and then release the mouse.

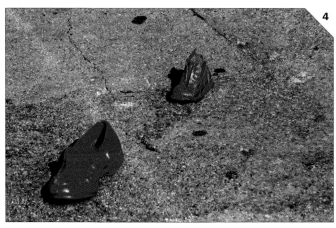

1 In this example, we are going to use the Patch tool to remove the last and smallest of these three red shoes in the image.

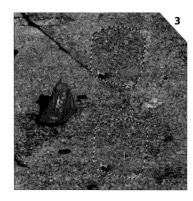

2 With the Patch tool selected, draw around the object you want to remove. Once you've done this, the selection will change to the familiar dotted line, or 'marching ants'.

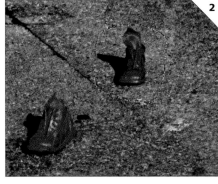

4 Photoshop will sample the new area onto which you dragged the selection and use it to replace the initial area.

How effective the result is depends on the complexity of both the selected area and the sample area. Here, the random pattern of the road has resulted in a pretty convincing fix.

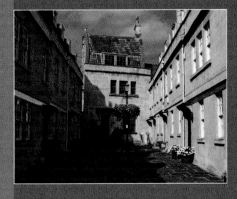 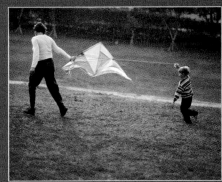 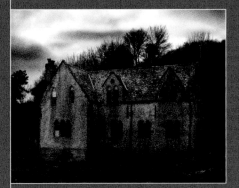

2

Advanced Image Editing

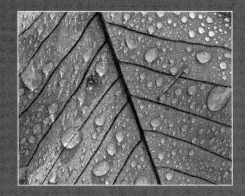 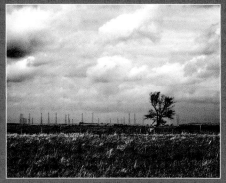 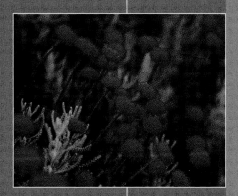

Modern image-editing applications have much to offer in terms of image enhancement. Most software works on a layer-based system, allowing you to make localized or wholesale adjustments to an image without affecting the original. Using layers and controlling how they interact with each other by applying a variety of blending options, along with a vast array of editing tools and creative filters, opens up endless possibilities for your images – a virtual world in which your imagination is given an entirely free rein. Chapter 2 introduces some of the possibilities. It's by no means exhaustive, but you should be given all the information you need to continue exploring for yourself.

Introducing Layers

Layers were introduced with the third version of Photoshop, Photoshop 3. Their introduction turned image-editing software on its head. Layers make editing images much easier than if you have to work on a traditional single-layered canvas. They allow you to do things that would be impossible with a traditional 'one-layer' canvas.

The concept often employed to explain how layers work is that of a stack of transparent sheets, such as those you use on an overhead projector. Although you begin with a single layer (often called the Background layer) you can create a new, empty, transparent layer above it, as if slipping a new transparency on top of the original stack on the projector. This enables you to draw on the new layer, on top of the background layer, without actually altering the background itself. You can slide the sheet around to move the new elements relative to whatever is on the background, which will remain unaltered. You can keep adding new layers whenever you want. Most image-editing software now supports layers; here, Photoshop was used to illustrate the concept.

BASIC LAYER CONSTRUCTION

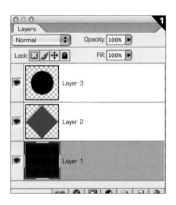 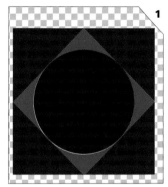

1 Here is a very basic three-layered visual construction of a circle, a diamond and a square. Each of the three elements was drawn on its own unique layer by selecting Layer>New. Each newly created layer will sit 'on top of', or 'in front of', the previous layer.

The corresponding Layers palette to the left of the illustration shows how one layer actually 'sits' on top of (or in front of) another. The Layers palette shows that the red 'background' square sits below a yellow diamond on which is placed a blue circle.

Note: visibility eye disappears

2 By clicking the 'Visibility eye' next to the Layer thumbnail in the Layers palette, it is possible to turn specific layers 'on' and 'off', making them visible or invisible. Here, clicking the Visibility eye next to the yellow diamond Layer thumbnail has rendered that layer invisible, leaving only the red square and the blue circle. Being able to turn layers 'on' and 'off' can help you to appraise images before and after an adjustment has been made.

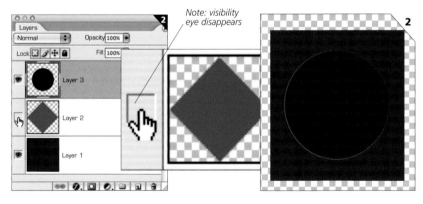

3 Here, the blue circle layer (Layer 3) has been turned off by again clicking on the Visibility eye, leaving only the red square and the yellow diamond visible. Not only do layers behave independently of one another, allowing you to apply adjustments to individual layers as opposed to the entire image, but you can also change their order simply by clicking and dragging the layers around in the Layers palette. This is shown in the next step, Step 4.

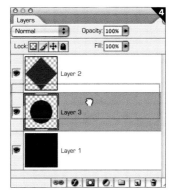
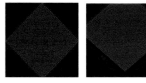

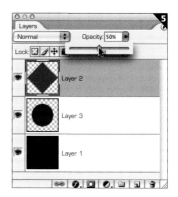

4 In the image above right, the blue circle layer has been dragged underneath (or behind) the yellow diamond layer. As you can see, the diamond totally covers up the blue circle. However, as an illustrative exercise, the three-dimensional image shows how the blue circle is actually hiding underneath the diamond.

Unlike transparent sheets on a projector, digital layers are genuinely transparent, so no matter how many layers you add, the layers beneath will always remain sharp and clear. Digital layers differ in other ways, too: for example, it is possible to adjust the transparency – or 'Opacity' – of the elements. This allows elements on a 'lower' layer to start to appear through the upper layer. How visible they become depends on how transparent you make the layer above.

5 Using the Opacity slider to reduce the transparency of the yellow diamond layer allows the blue circle to start showing through the layer. Notice, however, that in reducing the opacity of the diamond layer, the saturation has also been 'weakened', draining it of its yellow colour. Wherever it interacts with another

colour, such as the red and the blue, a fourth and fifth colour are created.

The way that the hue, saturation and brightness values of individual pixels on one layer react with the corresponding pixels on another layer is governed by Blending Modes, another powerful feature of many software-editing programs, and usually found in the Layers palette. For more information on Blending Modes and how they work, turn to pages 40–1.

LAYERS IN PRACTICE

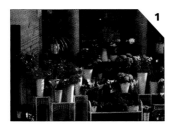
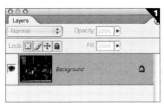

1 When you open an image in Photoshop, it's just like a normal photograph or artist's canvas. There's a single layer (called the Background layer), onto which you can draw or paint directly, or otherwise alter, using any of the editing tools. The heart of layers in most image-editing software is the Layers palette, which shows you all the layers that you have in your document.

2 Duplicate the background layer by creating a copy. You can do this in several ways, but the easiest is to drag the Background layer onto the 'Create a new layer' icon, which is at the top of the Layers palette.

Alternatively, go to Layer > Duplicate Layer. You can now safely edit a copy of the image, while keeping the original background layer intact. In this example, desaturate the duplicate layer by going to Image > Adjustments > Desaturate.

It's good to get into the habit of giving your layers names, as this will help you track your editing. Simply right-click/double-click in order to highlight the relevant layer text in the Layers palette and type in the new name.

3 A simple way to exploit layers is to remove parts of upper layers to allow layers below to show through. Select the Eraser tool and delete around half of the black and white layer to let the original colour layer show through. When happy with the result, go to Layer > Flatten Image. All the layers will be combined onto one layer to keep file sizes down.

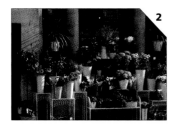

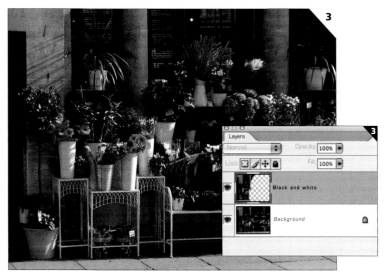

Using Layers

Having learned the basic concept of layers, and seen how by duplicating and altering the background layer you can create some interesting effects, let's see what happens when you combine two or more images to create one composite image. This could be the familiar photomontage type of composite, where images blend into one another to create a surreal piece of art, or when two or more images are combined to create an entirely believable scene. Here, using Photoshop Elements (but again other software will work in much the same way), we're going to replace the sky in one image with that from another, resulting in the creation of a new atmospheric shot. Replacing an uninteresting sky from a picture taken during an overcast day with a clear blue sky from another image is a common advertising trick.

COMBINING IMAGES USING LAYERS

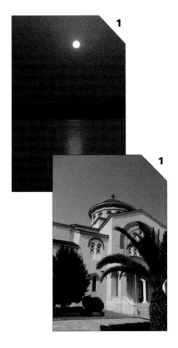

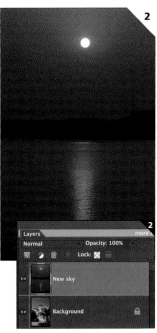

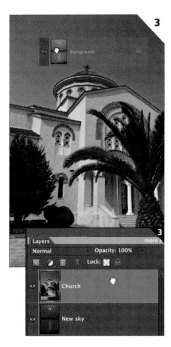

4 Use the Magic Wand tool to select the blue sky above the church. If it doesn't select all of the sky, hold down the Shift key and click on those regions that were missed. This will add them to the selection. Now, once you've selected the sky, go to Select > Feather and enter a value of 1 to soften the edges of the church so that they will blend more realistically with the sky. Press the Backspace key to delete the blue sky.

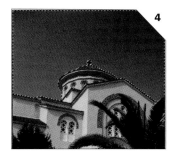

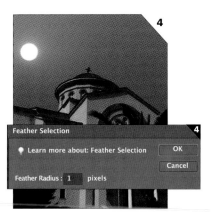

1 Here are the two source images – one of a Greek Orthodox church under a clear blue sky, and the other of a late afternoon sun. The images are very different in mood, colour and camera angle, but combining them using layers is a relatively quick and easy exercise. The more uniform the sky you want to replace is in tone and colour, the easier it is to cut out of the image using the Magic Wand tool. You should bear this in mind when selecting potential images for sky replacement.

2 Start by combining the two images into a single document. In the Layers palette, click and drag the background thumbnail image of one photograph and drop it into the canvas of the other image. A border appears around the image to indicate you can drop it, and holding down the Shift key will ensure the image is centred. Here, the sunset has been dragged onto the church image, covering it entirely. However, the Layers palette indicates there are two images.

3 Right-clicking/double-clicking on the Background layer of the church file allows you to convert it into a normal floating layer so that you can change the layer order. Unless you do this, you won't be able to move the Background layer, as it is locked.

Photoshop Elements will ask you if you want to give the new layer a name. Call it 'Church'. Drag the church layer above the sky so that it is now the uppermost layer in the Layers palette and covers the sky image.

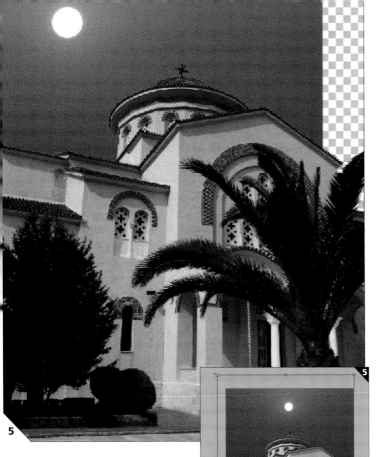

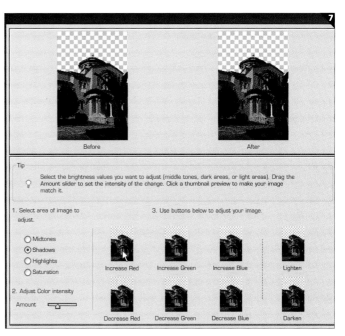

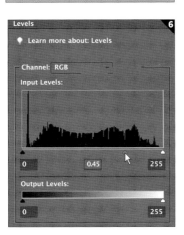

5 Now you need to move the sun a little to the left, so it's in line with the shadows on the church. To do this, you have to make the New sky layer a bit bigger, or there won't be enough sky on the right-hand side. Go to the Layers palette and select the New sky layer. In the Tool Options bar at the top of the screen, ensure Show Transform Controls is checked. This puts a box around the layer with eight rescale boxes – four at each corner, and four in the middle of each side. You'll have to zoom out to see these more clearly, which you can do by going to View > Zoom Out. Repeat the command until you can view the entire area, then resize the viewing window. Making sure 'Constrain Proportions' is checked in the Tool Options bar, grab one of the corners and rescale the sunset sky so that it is large enough to move to the left. Use the Move tool to reposition it.

6 You need to make the building and sky blend more closely in terms of tone and coloration. With the church layer selected, go to Image > Adjustments > Levels to open the Levels dialog window. Move the centre gamma (or grey) point to the right to darken the image of the church.

7 To adjust the colour of the church so that it matches the sunset sky, go to Image > Adjustments > Variations and click on Increase Red to warm the image.

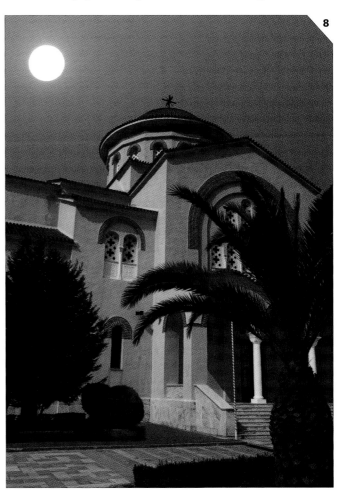

8 Here, you can see the successful final result. Simply by slightly repositioning the sun to the left, and getting the church to match the colour and brightness of the sky, it has been possible to create a believable and atmospheric image, using only two layers.

Adjustment Layers

Image-editing adjustments can enhance dull pictures and give you the creative control to overcome problems with lighting, colour casts or even exposure. Unfortunately, there is a catch. Once you've applied such adjustments, they can be difficult or even impossible to reverse, and if you apply several adjustments one after another, you may degrade image quality. However, many editing applications offer a way of applying adjustments that, while affecting how the image looks, actually reside on a separate layer. Using these 'adjustment' layers allows you to apply the entire range of editing tools and commands without affecting the background image. In this way, you can work on an image, applying brightness, colour and tonal corrections, which you can later go back and adjust or delete entirely, if you like. Here, we're using Photoshop Elements to show how versatile adjustment layers are.

CONTROLLING THE IMAGE ENVIRONMENT

1 Open the image you want to edit. Here, we're going to turn this daytime shot into a brightly lit night shot. Go to Layer > New Adjustment Layer to see a submenu of layer adjustments that can be applied in this way. Choosing an adjustment brings up a dialog box that allows you to give your adjustment layer a name. If you're making a lot of changes to a photograph, or want to create a multi-layer composition, it pays to remind yourself of the purpose of each layer by giving it a name.

Like other layers, an adjustment layer has its own Blending Mode and Opacity. You can leave these at the default settings for now, as you can always go back and adjust them at a later stage.

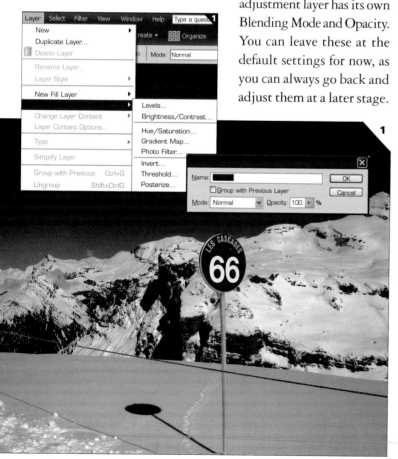

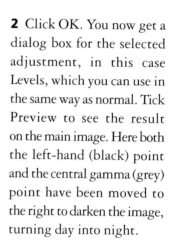

2 Click OK. You now get a dialog box for the selected adjustment, in this case Levels, which you can use in the same way as normal. Tick Preview to see the result on the main image. Here both the left-hand (black) point and the central gamma (grey) point have been moved to the right to darken the image, turning day into night.

3 When you click OK, the adjustment is applied to your image, but it isn't applied directly. If you look in the Layers palette, you will see that you've created a separate layer containing the adjustment, with the name you applied in Step 1. Hide this by clicking on the Eye icon to the left of its name. The original image is then revealed, unaltered.

While the adjustment layer is selected, you can click the Opacity drop-down menu at the top of the Layers palette to reduce the strength of the adjustment. Do this by dragging the slider. If you change your mind about the adjustment made, double-

click the thumbnail at the far left of the layer name, which depicts the adjustment. In this case, a histogram for Levels is shown. The Levels dialog is reopened, allowing you to fine-tune the settings. To remove the adjustment altogether, delete the layer.

Because the adjustment is applied to the image 'live', you can add as many adjustment layers as you like, and change them as often as necessary, without any cumulative degradation in image quality.

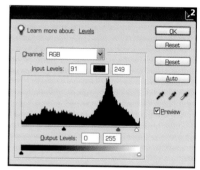

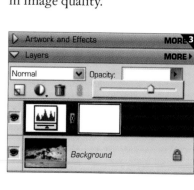

4 The thumbnail to the right of the Adjustment layer thumbnail represents a layer mask. By default this is white, which indicates that the adjustment applies to the whole image.

To apply an adjustment layer to a limited area of an image, first create a selection. Here, the sky has been isolated using the Magic Wand tool. If you've already added an adjustment layer, remember to select the Background (or whichever layer contains your image) in the Layers palette before creating the selection, then switch back to the top layer so that your new adjustment will appear above this.

Now, go to Layer > New Adjustment Layer and select the required adjustment. A Hue/Saturation layer is used here to knock back the sky. The Hue is shifted to the left to make the blue of the sky colder, while the Saturation is reduced to make the blue less vivid, and Lightness is increased to match the tone with the snow in the lower part of the image, balancing the composition better.

5 Click OK to create your masked adjustment layer. In the Layers palette, the Mask thumbnail shows the area the adjustment is applied to in white, and the rest in black. For more information on how to use layer masks, go to pages 50–1.

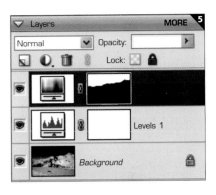

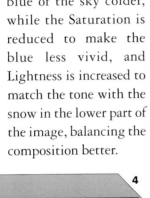

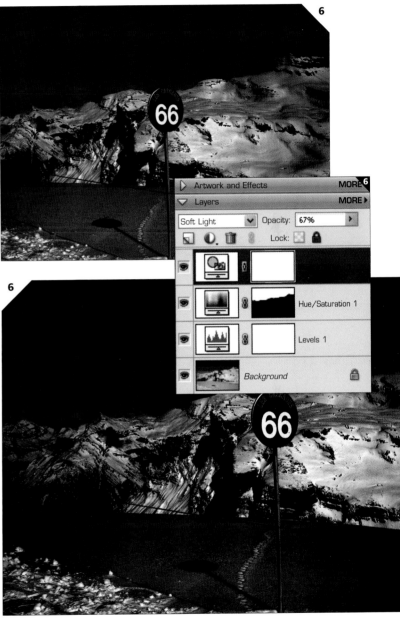

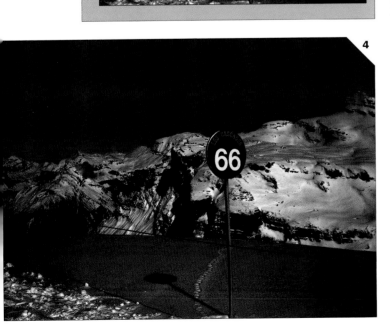

6 You can also use an adjustment layer's Blending Mode to alter its effect. Here, a blue tint has been added to the whole image using Layer > New Adjustment Layer > Photo Tint. The resulting artificial monochrome look isn't entirely satisfactory. In the Layers palette, changing the Photo Tint adjustment layer's Blending Mode from Normal to Soft Light helps to increase the contrast while preserving more of the underlying colour. Reducing the Opacity also helps to control the effect.

Blending Modes

In the last project we saw how altering the Blending Mode of an adjustment layer changes its effect on an image, but Blending Modes can be used for lots of other purposes, too. Every layer has a Blending Mode, which by default is Normal, meaning that anything in the layer covers up what's on the layer beneath. Again, most editing programs offer Blending Modes; here, we're going to use Photoshop to walk through some practical examples.

ADJUSTING TONAL AND COLOUR VALUES

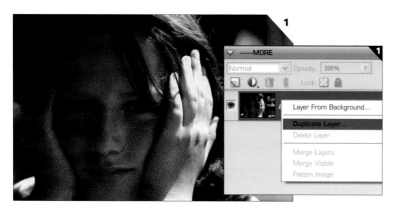

1 To use Blending Modes, you'll need an image with more than one layer. In photography, a useful way to exploit Blending Modes is to copy a single image onto itself and adjust the uppermost image.

Open your photograph and go to the Layers palette. Right-click/double-click on the Background layer and choose Duplicate Layer from the menu. In the dialog box, rename the new layer, or just click OK.

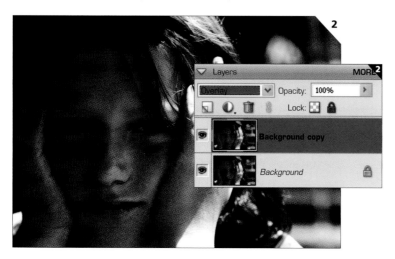

2 The blending mode of the current layer is shown in the drop-down menu at the top left of the Layers palette. Try changing it from Normal to Overlay. This serves to intensify the image, making the shadows darker, highlights lighter, and colours more saturated. This also gives the image a 'contrasty' fashion-photography look.

3 For an even 'hotter' look, try choosing Color Dodge. This brightens the image by increasing contrast and giving it greater colour saturation. With portrait photographs, which typically contain red and yellow tones, the result is reminiscent of a shot taken under intense sunlight. You can also still use the Opacity slider to reduce the effect of the blending mode layer.

4 For a quick soft-focus effect, use Gaussian Blur (Filter > Blur > Gaussian Blur) with a large Radius – in the case of this high-resolution close-up shot, it is 24 pixels – which will soften the layer. With Blending Modes such as those mentioned above, underlying detail still shows through, while low-contrast areas, such as skin texture, are smoothed out.

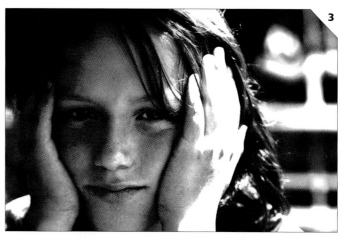

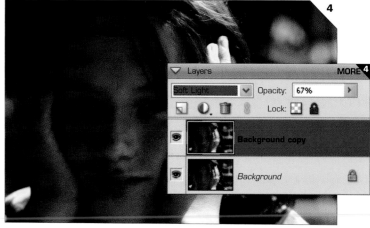

5 Blending Modes can also be used to help you combine images. In this example, a thought bubble has been added to a new layer using the Custom Shape tool and its Opacity has been reduced to allow the image below to show through. We now want to add an image scanned from a child's drawing.

6 In the Normal blending mode, the white paper covers the image and the bubble. Switching to Multiply superimposes the drawing on the bubble, as intended.

Blending modes explained

Understanding Blending Modes will help you to choose the correct ones when it comes to editing your images. A standard colour image stores red, green and blue (RGB) numbers for each pixel, giving each one a value from 0 to 255. This set of numbers is the pixel's colour value. In a layer blend, the colour value of the pixel in the layer is the 'blend colour'. The value of the pixel in the image as it was before the layer was added is the 'base colour'. A mathematical operation is applied to these values, producing a 'result colour'.

Two of the basic blend modes are Multiply and Screen. Adding a layer in Multiply mode simulates placing two slides in front of a projector's lamp at the same time. Both block some light, so the combined image is darker. Multiply works by multiplying the base and blend colours, then dividing by the maximum value of 255. For example, if you're layering an image on itself, and the R (red) value of a pixel is 100, the result will be (100x100)/255 = 39.

Screen mode does the inverse of this, resulting in a lighter image. Overlay mode combines Multiply and Screen. Where the base colour is dark, Multiply is applied, and where the base is light, Screen is applied. The result is a marked increase in contrast.

Blending modes are grouped by those that lighten an image, those that darken an image and those that do both. These groupings also tell you the neutral colour for each mode. When darkening, any pure white in the layer will leave the underlying image unchanged. When lightening, the same is true of black. And with balanced modes, 50% grey is normally neutral.

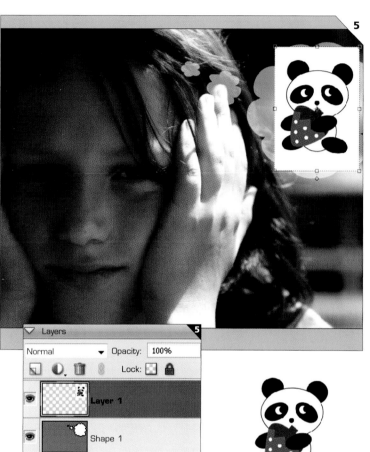

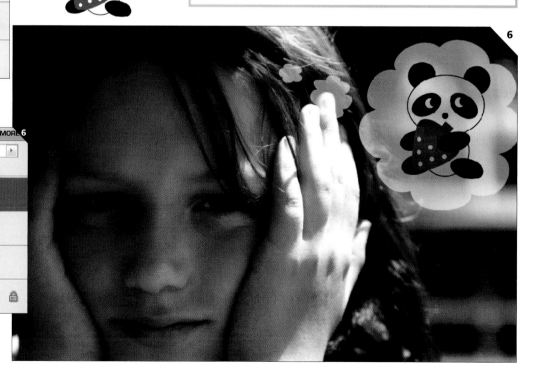

Merge for High Dynamic Range (HDR)

For many of you new to digital photography, the phrase 'Merge for HDR' may sound completely baffling, but in fact it's an easy concept to grasp and one that will potentially have an enormous effect on your photography.

Merge for HDR (High Dynamic Range) is simply a way of merging together a number of differently exposed images of the same scene in order to increase the dynamic range in a photograph. In the past, both film and digital cameras were only capable of capturing a set range of tones, and any tones outside of that range became either pure black or pure white, with no detail visible. However, a number of editing applications now allow you to merge several images that have been taken using different exposures, to capture a much greater range of tones. These all work in more or less the same way, but here we're going to use Photoshop's HDR merge feature.

MANIPULATING LIGHT LEVELS

1 This image of a modern building was shot on a sunny day. The sun was shining brightly on the right-hand side of the building, creating intense highlights on the windows and glass balconies, while the left-hand side of the building was in the shade. The result is an unevenly-lit photograph.

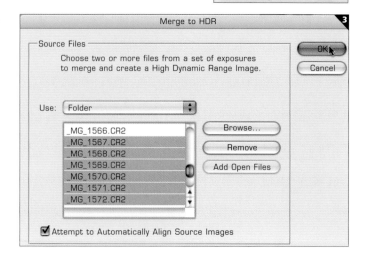

3 Go to File > Automate > Merge to HDR. The Merge to HDR dialog box will help you navigate to the folder and specific files you want to merge. There's no limit on the number of files, but five or six variously exposed images should achieve a high-dynamic range. Once you've selected the files, click OK.

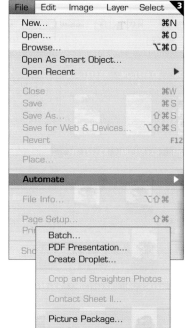

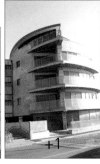
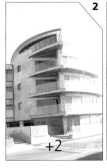
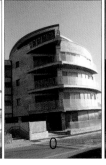
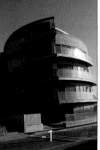
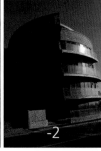

+2 +1 0 -1 -2

2 To fix this, first set the camera on a tripod and compose the shot. You need to take several images of the same scene, but at different exposures. It's possible to do this manually, by noting what an auto exposure would be, then setting the camera to manual. Start with the same exposure, then increase and decrease the aperture by 1 and 2 stops so that you have shots of the image at +2, +1, 0, -1, and -2 exposures. Alternatively, if your camera features Auto Bracketing, set it to +2/-2 and you will automatically take the same range of shots. The exact number of shots is not important, as long as you expose for all the highlights and shadows. You'll find the best results come if you shoot RAW. Download the images into one folder on to your computer.

4 Photoshop will now take some time to assess and merge the images. After a minute or so, the Merge to HDR dialog box will show your image with the various compensated exposures to the left. At this stage, the main image will probably look the same as one of the images to the left, because the monitor cannot show the image in 32-bit mode.

5 For the real benefit to be made apparent, go to Mode and select 8 Bits/Channel. Photoshop will bring up the HDR Conversion dialog box. This gives you four ways in which you can improve the conversion. Highlight Compression and Equalize Histogram apply automatic settings, but Exposure and Gamma and Local Adaptation

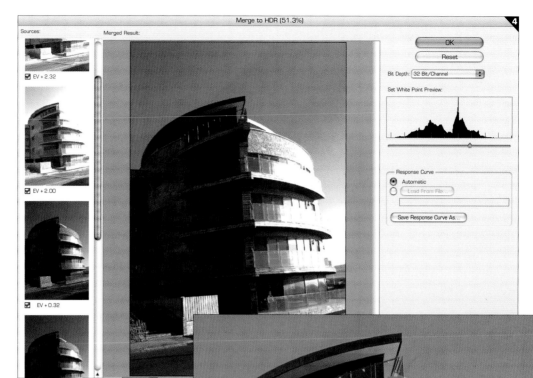

will allow you to make manual adjustments and provide the best level of control. Each image will be different, so experiment with all four options.

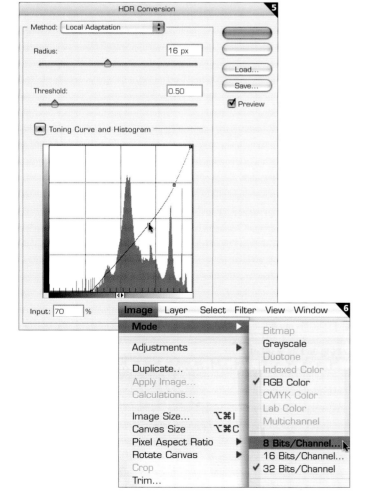

6 Once you've extracted the best tonal range from the image, go to Mode and convert the image from 16 Bits/Channel (which it will have automatically defaulted to) to 8 Bits/Channel. You will now be able to make further changes to colour and tone using the conventional editing commands.

Merge to HDR can often produce unrealistic-looking images, and it's often quite easy to spot an image that has undergone the process. However, there's no doubt that merging several images can create extraordinary results, with a coloration and tone that is unique to the HDR process.

Using the Selection Tools

Selections are crucial to precise image editing, no matter what application you're using. There are literally scores of ways to make selections, and which one you choose to use will depend on the nature of the area you want to select and the specific software you're using; here, we're using Photoshop Elements. Although each of the tools can be used independently, the real power comes when you combine a number of Selection tools to isolate the area you want. For example, the Magic Wand is great for selecting ranges of similar colours, while the Marquee tools are very effective for selecting discrete islands of pixels, regardless of what colour they are. Using the Add or Subtract options, you can use the Marquee or Lasso tool to clean up a selection made using the Magic Wand, or vice versa.

SELECTING TO ALTER ELEMENTS OF AN IMAGE

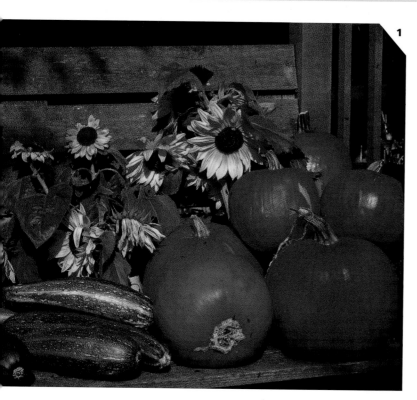

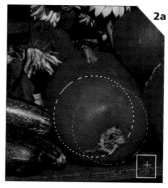

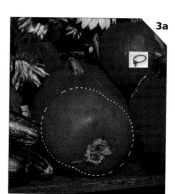

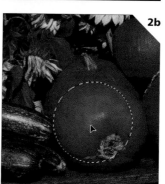

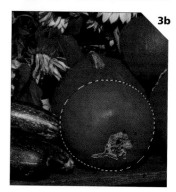

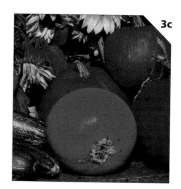

1 If you want to make a selection in an image such as this, there are a number of options. Let's run through a few simple ways of adding to selections that will help speed up the process.

2 One of the pumpkins at the bottom left is a slightly different colour to the rest, so let's start by making this pumpkin even more off-colour. A simple option is to use the Elliptical Marquee tool – clicking and dragging from the middle of the pumpkin while holding down the Shift key to drag out from the centre will automatically create a perfectly round selection. You can move the selection by dragging inside it, and using Shift (to add) and Alt (to subtract) to fine-tune the selection, dragging out additional areas to add to or cut away from the current selection.

3 With the outline shape of the pumpkin selected, holding down the Alt key while using the Lasso tool (a small '-' minus sign will appear next to the tool's cursor) allows you to draw around the woody, fibrous base of the pumpkin to deselect it.

Once the pumpkin has been accurately selected, we can use the Hue/Saturation command to radically alter the colour of the pumpkin.

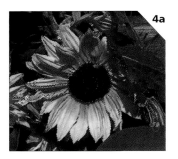

4a

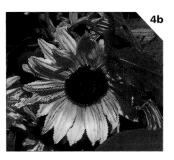

4b

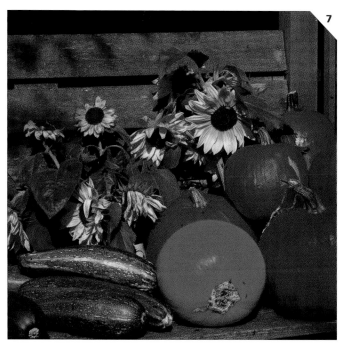

7

4 Next, let's turn to the Magic Wand tool to select a sunflower. Begin by moving the tool around and adding to the selection by holding down the Alt key. Note that if you inadvertently select a large unwanted area, switch to the Lasso tool and, with the Alt key held down, draw around the unwanted selection to deselect it.

5 Once the flower-head has been accurately selected, the Hue/Saturation command can again be used to change its colour.

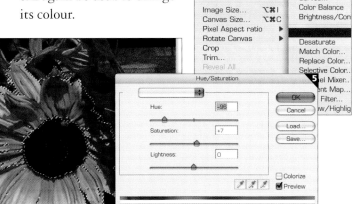

7 Having made the initial selection with the Magic Brush tool, the Lasso and Magnetic Lasso tools can be used to add to (by holding down Shift) or take away from (by holding down Alt) the selection. With the selection completed, that region of the picture can be recoloured.

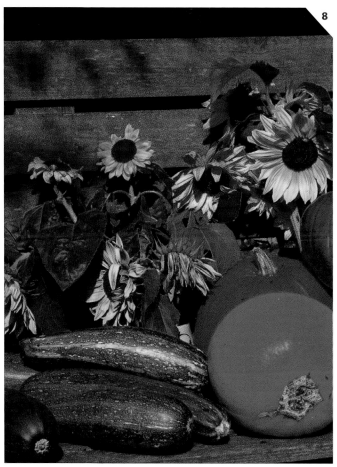

8

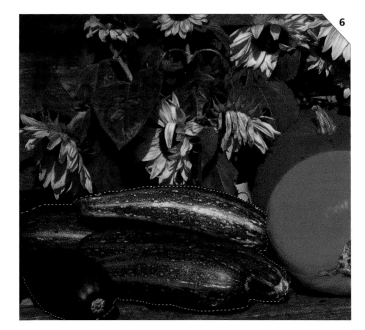

6

6 Next, try using the Magic Brush tool to make a rough selection around the courgettes (zucchini). If you don't have a version of the software that features the Magic Brush, then you can use one of the equivalent selection tools.

8 By using a variety of tools, and by adding to and subtracting from selections, it's surprisingly easy to make even the most difficult selections and arrive at a positively multicoloured collection of fruit and veg.

Making Cut-outs

One procedure that you may find you need to carry out from time to time – particularly if you're keen on creating photomontages, making composite images of family members or friends, or placing objects in front of different backgrounds – is to make accurate cut-outs. All editing software will have the necessary tools to create accurate, natural-looking cut-outs.

As always, there are a number of ways of performing cut-outs, some of which might involve the use of the Selection tools discussed on the previous pages. In this example, however, Photoshop Elements is used to create a 'mask' around the image to be cut out, as this offers the greatest control and allows the cut-out to be constantly revised until you're happy with it.

USING THE MASK TOOL FOR CUT-OUTS

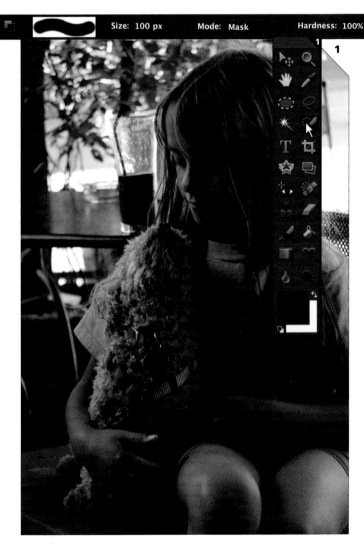

Size: 100 px   Mode: Mask   Hardness: 100%   Overlay: 50%

2 To begin with, click on the Selection Brush in the Toolbox. Programs other than Photoshop Elements may not include exactly the same tool, but you can usually use the Brush tool as a selection tool in the majority of programs. Go to the Tool Options bar at the top of the screen and select Mask in the Mode drop-down menu.

Elements will use a red colour to represent the mask as a default colour, a feature dating back to the days of conventional printing, when masks used to be cut out of a red acetate material that was known as Rubylith. If you're editing a photograph that is primarily red, the default mask colour makes it more difficult to see what you're doing, so simply click in the colour square and select a different colour for the mask.

It's also possible to change the Opacity of the mask, but for most editing jobs, leave it set to 100%.

3 Set Hardness to 100% initially, to ensure that there is a crisp edge. Adjust the size of the brush using the '[' and ']' keys, and begin painting the mask over the area you want to cut out. For large areas, where there's little risk of painting over the background, use a large brush, as this will speed up the job.

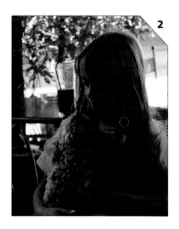

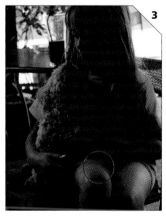

1 This image of a little girl and a dog presents an interesting array of problems in terms of creating an accurate cut-out. First, you will have to cut out around the hair of both the girl and the dog, which is notoriously difficult to deal with, and, second, the background is far from being uniform in colour, which makes it impossible to select using the Magic Wand tool.

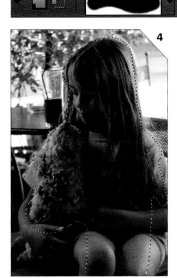

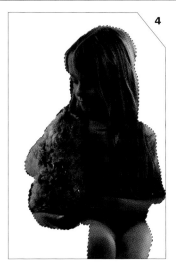

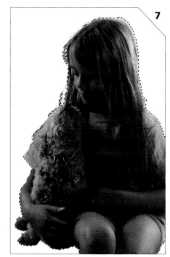

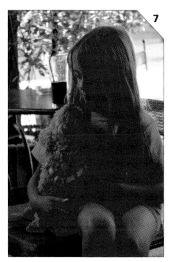

4 Although you're painting a mask, you are in effect making a selection at the same time.

To view the selection, go to the Tool Options bar and change the Mode from Mask to Selection. The familiar marching ants selection will appear. For this exercise, the Backspace/Delete key has been pressed to show how the mask is progressing. Click Edit > Undo to go back a step and bring back the background.

5 When you get to the more detailed areas, such as around the dog's coat, reduce the size of the brush so that you can trace the edges far more accurately.

You can also reduce the brush's Hardness value in the Tool Options bar. This creates a softer-edged brush, which means you will be able to soften the edges of the selection.

6 If you inadvertently paint over the background, simply hold down the Alt key and brush out the mask.

Zoom into the image as you go to refine the mask, using a very small brush to get into difficult areas.

7 Once you're happy with the mask, go to Filter > Gaussian Blur and blur the mask with a Radius of 0.5, just to soften the edges of it slightly.

Next, convert the mask back into a selection in the Tool Options bar. Here, the background has been deleted to leave the cut-out on a white layer.

8 Alternatively, you can copy the cut-out, and then paste it into a new document, where you can then create an entirely different background.

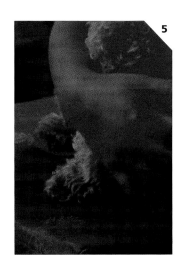

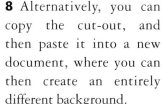

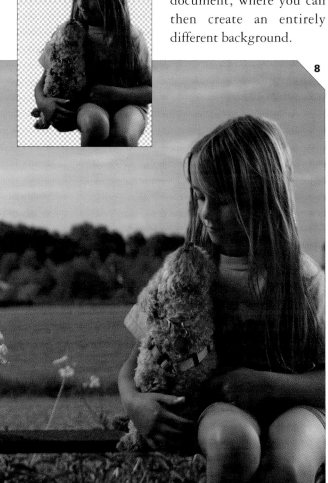

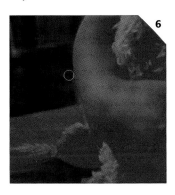

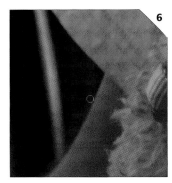

Creating Montages

Having learned how to make selections and accurate cut-outs of individual elements within an image, it's time to put all these skills together to make a photomontage. Using image-editing software to create a photomontage is much quicker and easier than using old photographs and a pair of scissors and, because you can blend images, the results are much more satisfactory. Before you start to create your montage, it's a good idea to place all the images that you're considering using in one readily identifiable folder so that you can access them quickly and easily. All editing software is capable of creating photomontages; here, we're using Photoshop.

COLLATING PHOTOMONTAGE ELEMENTS

1 The first image you select for your photomontage is the most important, as it will form the central point of your image, and set the scene in terms of subject and tone. This particular image has been chosen because it has plenty of space around the main subject into which new images can be added.

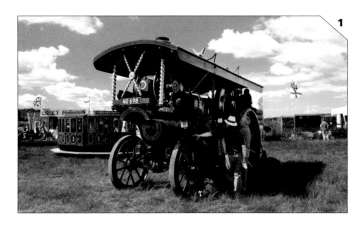

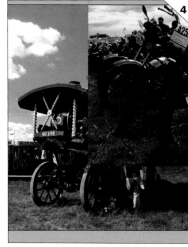

2 Open the second image and make any editing adjustments you need. You may have to adjust the crop, the sharpness, or adjust the brightness levels to try and ensure that it matches the first image as closely as possible. This is best done with both images on screen at the same time so you can get the best possible match.

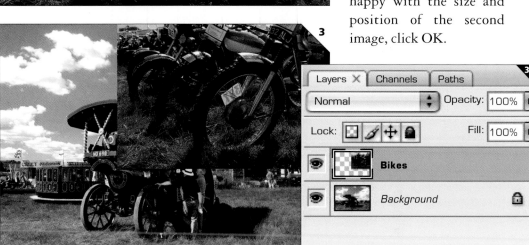

4 Ensuring that the 'Show Transform Controls' box is checked in the Tool Options bar, click on one of the corner boxes and, while holding down the Shift key to retain the image's proportions, rescale it to the size you want. When you're happy with the size and position of the second image, click OK.

3 Use the Move tool to drag the second image onto the first. In the Layers palette, you will see that the second image has been automatically created on a new layer. Give the layer an appropriate name so you can keep track of the various elements of the montage. In this example, we've labelled our layer 'Bikes'.

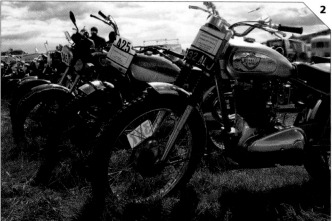

5 Go to the Toolbox and select the Eraser tool. In the Tool Options bar, set the Opacity to around 30% and use the '[' and ']' keys to select a suitable brush size. Carefully begin to rub out parts of the second image that you don't want to appear in the montage. Concentrate first on the edges, and remember that if you make a mistake you can always click Undo to undo the step.

6 Repeat the exercise with as many additional images as you like, remembering to give each new layer its own name in the Layers palette so you can keep track of the elements in your image.

7 When you have all your elements in place and you're happy with the composition, try experimenting with various Blending Modes and reducing the Opacity of some of the layers. This can add greater depth to the montage. Once you are satisfied with the way the piece is looking, go to Layers > Flatten Image before choosing Save to save the file on your hard drive.

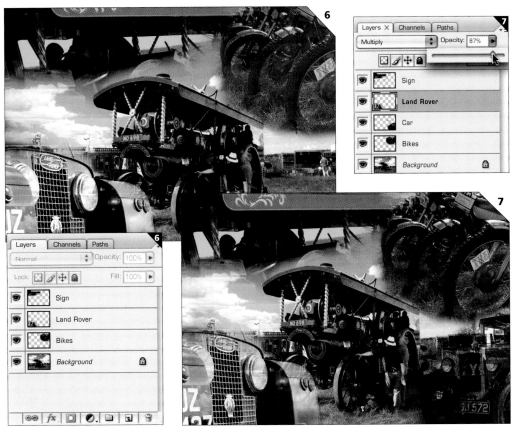

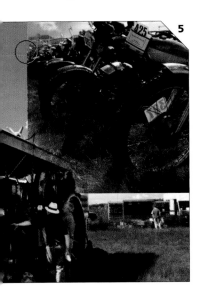

8 Given the subject matter of this montage, however, before we flattened the image, we used a Hue/Saturation adjustment layer to desaturate the colours by moving the Saturation slider to the left for a faded, slightly nostalgic feel. It also helps to unify the montage visually.

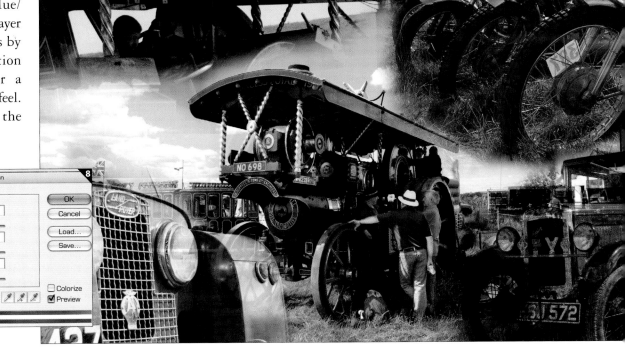

Layer Masks

A number of the more advanced image-editing programs have a powerful editing tool at their disposal, known as 'layer masks'. Creating a 'mask' was described previously, and the project here is a continuation of that in some ways. As we know, the term 'mask' derives from conventional printing where, in order for part of an image to remain unaffected by additional processes, a mask cut out of acetate was made to protect it. Digital layer masks work in much the same way, but are far more flexible. Here, we look at how layer masks can be used in Photoshop, or Photoshop Elements, although similar principles apply to most editing software.

USING LAYER MASKS TO ALTER IMAGES

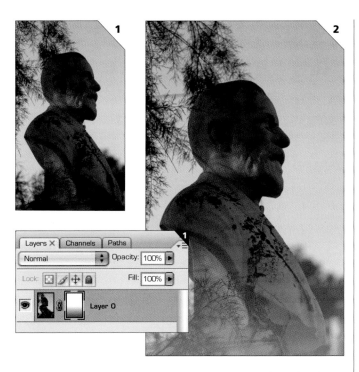

The aim here is to apply a simple mask to this image of a bust.

1 Go to the Layers palette and then begin by double-clicking the Background layer. It will ask if you'd like to rename the layer – click 'yes' to Layer 0. The reason why you have to do this is because a layer mask cannot be applied to the Background layer.

Click on 'Add layer mask' in the Layers palette. A white box will appear next to the image thumbnail.

2 Ensuring that the layer mask is active (it will have a double outline), return to the main image and draw a simple black gradient over the image. Part of the image will fade out. Looking at the Layers palette you'll see the part of the image that has faded out is represented by a fading black gradient in the Layer mask thumbnail.

Wherever black appears on the layer mask, the corresponding part of the image will be shown deleted (but it's still there until you flatten the image).

Let's apply this in a very simple 'real world' project. Here, the aim of the exercise is to mask the opening to this castle wall and replace the background.

1 Click on the 'Add layer mask' icon to create the mask. Return to the image and, with the Brush tool set to paint black, start to paint out the opening. Use a small, soft brush to paint the outline, and then fill the remainder with a larger brush, making sure Opacity is set to 100%. Looking at the Layer mask thumbnail in the Layers palette reflects where you've been painting.

2 Once the layer mask is complete, open the image for the replacement view and use the Move tool to drag it onto the main castle wall image.

In the Tool Options bar, ensure 'Show Transform Controls' is checked and then resize the new layer.

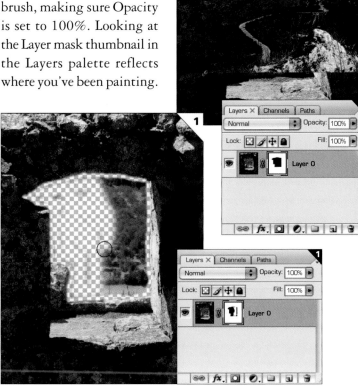

3 To get the new view to sit under the window, go to the Layers palette and move the new layer below Layer 0. You can independently edit the layers so they match in terms of tone and lighting. With the mask in place, it's easy to use any view you want.

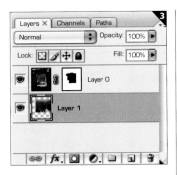

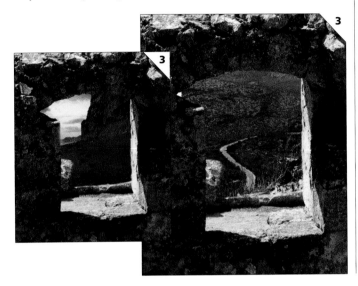

CREATING COMPOSITE LAYERS

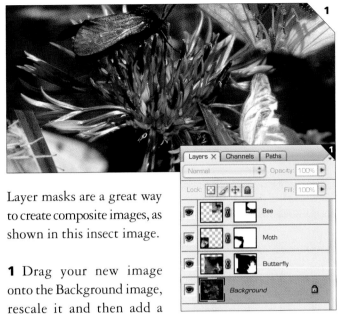

Layer masks are a great way to create composite images, as shown in this insect image.

1 Drag your new image onto the Background image, rescale it and then add a layer mask to each new layer. With the layer mask in place, paint with a black brush to reveal the layer underneath. Painting with a white brush reinstates any of the new layer that may have been removed.

ADJUSTMENT LAYERS AS LAYER MASKS

Photoshop Elements doesn't support layer masks in quite the same way. However, any new adjustment layer is automatically presented with its own layer mask, which can then be used in the way described previously.

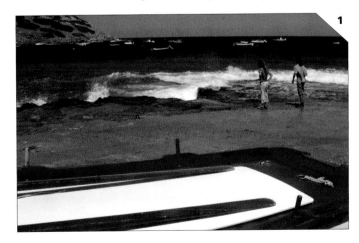

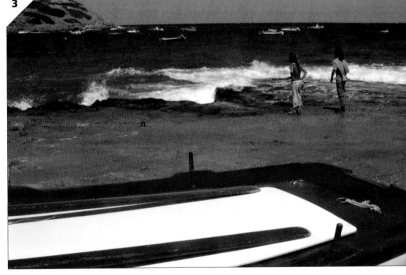

1 In this example, we're going to use the layer mask that comes with a Hue/Saturation adjustment layer to create an image in which parts are coloured a sepia tone while other parts remain in full colour.

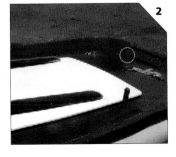

2 Having created a Hue/Saturation adjustment layer, clicked Colorize in the Hue/Saturation dialog window, and adjusted the sliders to create a sepia effect, the layer mask can now be selectively painted out using a white brush to reveal the colour underneath.

3 In a matter of moments, painting with white on the adjustment layer's layer mask has returned the foreground boat and distant figures to the original colour.

Meanwhile, the rest of the image has the sepia tone created by the Hue/Saturation adjustment layer.

Photoshop Filters

Photoshop and Photoshop Elements provide a huge variety of filters. These can alter an image in all manner of ways, from manipulating colours, adding textures, exaggerating or removing detail, picking out edges, simulating a painting or drawing, pinching or twisting the canvas, and more besides. You may not use them every day, but you can have endless fun exploring the creative possibilities.

One thing to remember with Filters is that the lower the resolution of the image, the greater the effect of the filter. The Filter Gallery provides a special user interface for many of the filters, with a large preview panel that you can enlarge further by expanding the window. The round button with two chevrons, to the left of the OK button, shows or hides the filters list, which also provides thumbnails to illustrate each effect. Using the Gallery is the best way to familiarize yourself with the filter names and their corresponding effects. Here is a small selection of available filters.

Posterize

The filters in the first group, Adjustments, are the simplest. Posterize, for example, simply reduces the number of colours in the image. Adjust the number of Levels for the desired effect, which is typically reminiscent of garish low-quality reproduction, as in Pop Art.

Cut-out

The Artistic filter set is slightly more sophisticated, with multiple sliders that give greater control over the results. The default settings often work well enough, however.

The Cut-out filter divides an image into areas of flat colour. Here settings of 5 Levels, Edge Simplicity 4 and Edge Fidelity 2 were used.

Film grain

Filters don't only (or always) do what they claim to do. Film Grain, for example, is at its most effective when used to simulate bad printing rather than grainy film.

Set the Intensity and Grain to high values, then increase the Highlight Area to restore image brightness at the expense of detail.

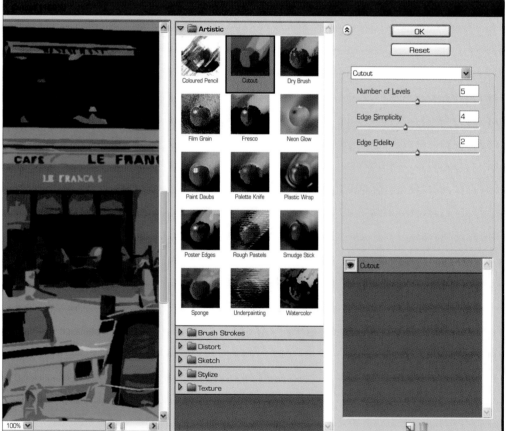

Gallery page

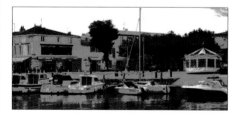

Posterize

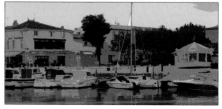

Cut-out

Film grain

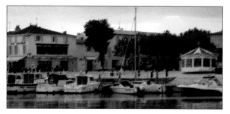

Rough pastels

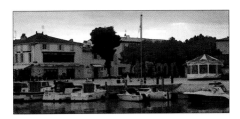

Accented edges

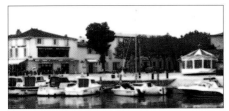

Diffuse glow

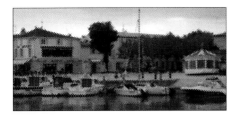

Glass

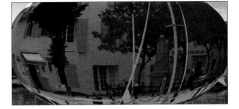

Spherize

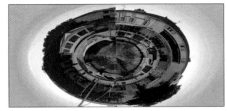

Polar coordinates

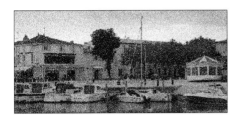

Pointillize

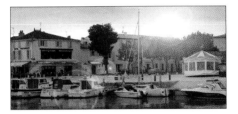

Lens flare

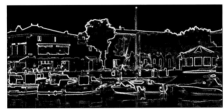

Glowing edges

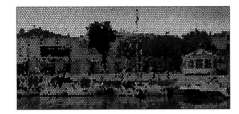

Stained glass

Rough pastels

Look out for Size, Length or Scaling settings, as these will need to be adjusted according to the resolution of your image. Here, the filter has been used with Stroke Length 17 and Canvas Texture 166%.

Accented edges

Several filters emphasize edges. Accented Edges (under Brush Strokes) is one of the more versatile, and demands more slider fiddling. At its best, it will mimic a pen and watercolour sketch.

Diffuse glow

The Distort filters serve disparate purposes. Diffuse Glow is a distortion filter because it shifts pixels, but its purpose is to create a soft-focus effect. Increase Glow Amount for a stronger effect, and increase Clear Amount to restore detail.

Glass

At low settings, with the Frosted Texture selected, the Glass filter puts your image behind sandblasted glass.

Adjust the Scaling to suit the image size, or switch the texture to Tiny Lens and increase the settings.

Spherize

The distortion filters can be great fun to use. Apply the spherize filter with a positive value to create a fishbowl effect. The maximum 100% setting isn't all that strong, so try applying it more than once. A small negative setting can be useful for countering wide-angle lens distortion.

Polar coordinates

The most extreme of the distortion filters is proabably Polar Coordinates. A good tip is to rotate a landscape image 180% (that is, turn it upside down) before applying Rectangular to Polar. Try this on a panoramic landscape with a dark sky, then layer a picture of the Earth in the middle.

Pointillize

The Pixelate filters break images into colour cells. Pointillize mimics the 'pointillism' technique of the Impressionist painter Georges Seurat.

Lens flare

The Render filters are among the most sophisticated. Lens Flare simulates the rings that are produced by shooting toward the sun or a strong light source. Click to align the centre of the flare with the source, and choose a lens type to set the size and appearance of the flare.

Glowing edges

The Sketch filters are intended to work with hard-edged images, and often draw a blank with detailed images. More rewarding are the Stylize filters, which include Extrude, and are worth trying. Glowing Edges turns any image into neon, but keep the Smoothness setting high.

Stained glass

Texture is an intriguing set of filters. The Stained Glass option creates white leading instead of black. To fix this, invert your image, then go to Filter > Texture > Stained Glass, set the Light Intensity to 0, adjust the other sliders as you like, click OK, then invert again.

Dramatic Skies

One of the key elements of many successful landscape photographs is a sky that, without detracting from the remainder of the image, can grab and hold the viewer's attention and add to the overall atmosphere of the image – whether it comprises forbidding, stormy rain clouds or a clear, unadulterated, azure blue.

However, setting the correct exposure for both sky and land is sometimes impossible, especially if your camera cannot be fitted with a grey graduated filter, commonly known as a grey grad filter. These filters are tinted at the top and gradually fade to clear at the bottom, and are designed to prevent a sky being overexposed when the photographer has set the correct exposure for the land. However, it is mainly only dSLRs and some hybrid cameras that accept such filters, and not every dSLR owner carries them around at all times.

However, as long as you can manage to stop the sky from 'blowing out' altogether, and retain most of the detail, you can enhance the sky in your image-editing software and recreate the effect of a grey grad filter.

ENHANCE LIGHTING WITH GRAD FILTERS

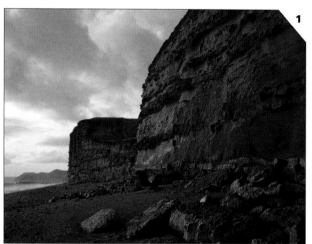

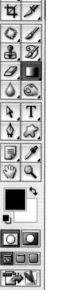

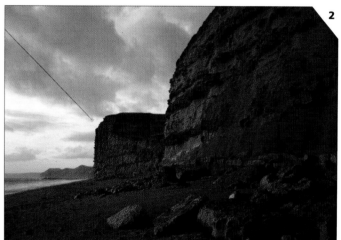

1 Although there isn't a dramatic difference in light levels between the sky and the land in this image, a grey grad filter would have brought out more depth in the clouds and given them a little more body.

2 To recreate the grey grad effect, begin by creating a new blank layer (Layer > New > Layer) and call it Gradient. Ensure the Foreground/ Background colours in the Toolbar are set to the default of black as the foreground colour and white as the background colour. Now, select the Gradient tool in the Toolbar and in the Tool Options bar select the 'Foreground to Transparent' gradient option.

Next, draw a line across the sky. You will see that the line runs diagonally from the top left of the image to the start of the cliffs.

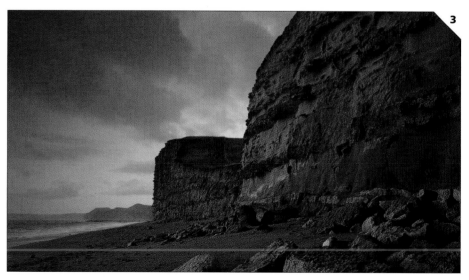

3 After releasing the mouse, the area along the gradient line will darken. This is the result of creating a black-to-transparent gradient over the original image. Experiment with the length of the gradient line to see how it influences how much of the image is affected.

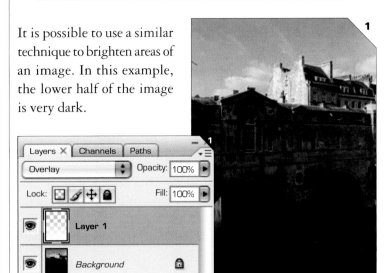

BRIGHTEN DARKENED AREAS

It is possible to use a similar technique to brighten areas of an image. In this example, the lower half of the image is very dark.

4 To complete the grey grad effect, go to the Layers palette. Ensure the Gradient layer is selected and change the Blending Mode to Overlay. The background clouds will now blend into the dark grey gradient and become darker.

1 As before, create a new blank layer, but this time choose white as the foreground colour instead of black before you draw the gradient rule. To do this, simply click on the right-angled arrow icon to switch between the two colours. If the foreground and background colours are anything but black and white, simply press the 'D' key (for 'default'). As before, change the gradient layer's Blending Mode to Overlay.

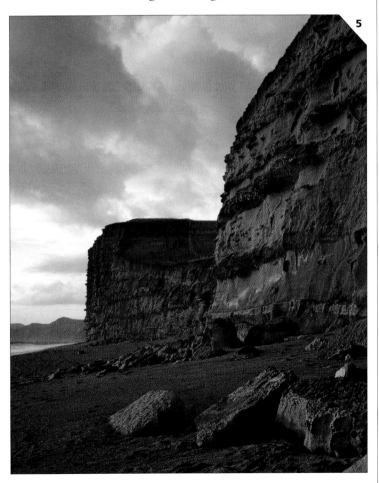

5 You can temper the effect of the gradient by reducing the Opacity of the Gradient layer. With this image, however, the sky could be enhanced further, so the Gradient layer has been duplicated, doubling the effect it has on the image.

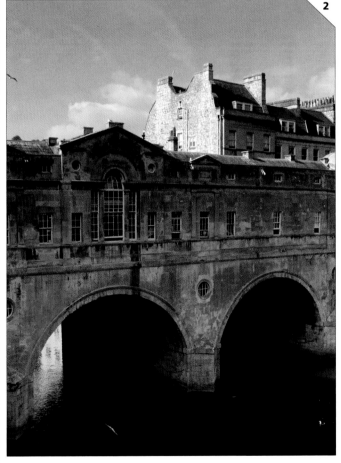

2 With the white gradient layer set to Overlay, the water and lower part of the building are dramatically brightened.

Black and White Conversion

Creating good black and white images from your colour originals is not as easy as it sounds. You might think that all you have to do is remove the colour information in the digital image, and technically that is precisely what you do to get an essentially greyscale image.

Artistically, however, the results of such a simple process are rarely as good as you'd expect without some digital tweaking along the way. Part of the reason for this is that photographers have long used coloured filters to alter the image before it's captured on black and white film. Different coloured filters cause different objects or areas to be brighter or darker when photographed, depending on their colour.

This is important, because although certain objects, such as grass and sky, are different colours, their brightness may actually be very similar. This can result in a 'flat' black and white image, where similar areas merge together unless a filter is used on the lens. But rather than spend money on filters, you can replicate the effect in Photoshop.

REPLICATING FILTERS IN PHOTOSHOP

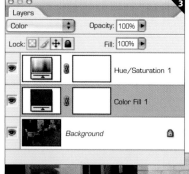

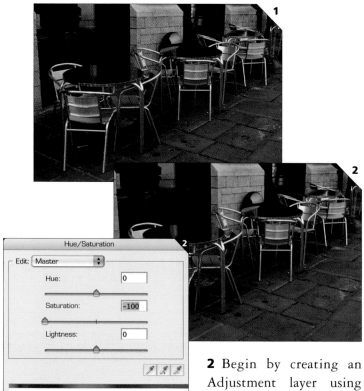

1 Here's the original colour image that we want to try and convert into a black and white photograph. There's not a lot of strong colour in the shot to start with, as the pavement, tables and doors are all neutral colours. This makes it more of a challenge to convert it successfully into a black and white image.

2 Begin by creating an Adjustment layer using Hue/Saturation to remove the colour information from the image. Set the Saturation slider to -100 to do this.

While the colour has gone, the image now looks dull and lacks contrast – this is often described as 'flat'. Now, the dark pavement dominates the picture, and the chairs and tables appear a little lost against it.

3 Just as a photographer uses coloured lens filters to adjust the brightness of the objects in the scene in relation to one another, you can prefilter the image before it is desaturated. To do this, simply create a new layer above the background layer and then fill it with a solid colour. With the background layer selected in the Layers palette go to Layer > New Fill Layer > Solid Color and click OK. In the subsequent Colour Picker box, choose an appropriate colour. Here, an electric blue has been selected. Set the Layer Blending mode of the Color Fill layer to Color. The image becomes washed out, but the pavement is now much lighter.

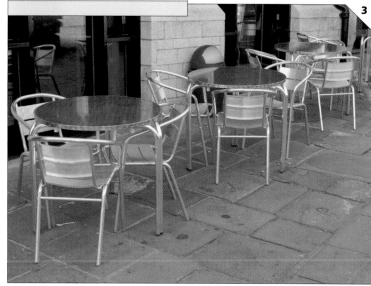

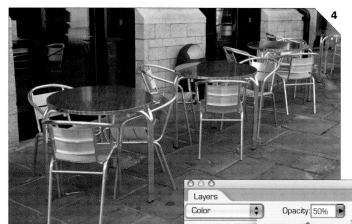

5 By adding a Brightness/ Contrast Adjustment layer above the Hue/Saturation layer, you can add some contrast to the image.

Move the Contrast slider to the right until you get the appearance that you want. The resulting image is a much snappier conversion and the tables really stand out from the pavement.

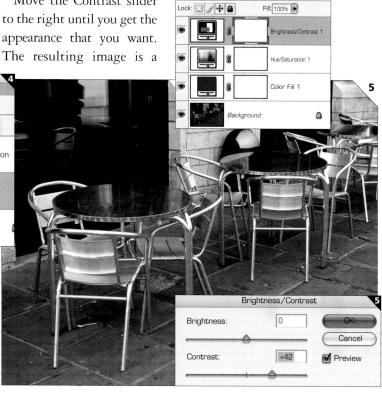

4 You can adjust different colours in the image by changing the Hue of the Color Fill layer. This is like changing the filter on a lens.

In the Layers palette, Right-click/Double-click the Layer thumbnail on the Color Fill layer.

Make sure that H is selected in the HSB section of the Color Picker and drag the slider to adjust the hue of the colour filter. This will change the relationship between the various tones.

Here, the Color Layer Opacity has been reduced to 50%, so the effect does not appear as strong.

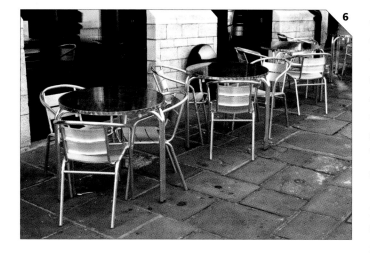

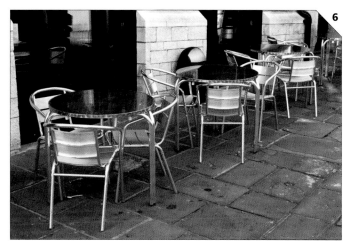

6 The advantage of working with adjustment layers is that you can go back and edit each adjustment at a later stage. In fact, you can even save documents as Photoshop (.psd) or TIFF (.tif) files with the adjustment layers in place.

The only instance when you can't go back and alter an adjustment layer is once you've flattened an image. This is usually used as a way of keeping the file size down and is done by selecting Layer > Flatten Image.

In the two images shown here, the Hue/Saturation dialog window was activated by Right-clicking/Double-clicking the Hue/Saturation Adjustment layer in the Layers palette. Checking the Colorize button and also altering the Hue and Saturation sliders will adjust the colour as well as the intensity of the image.

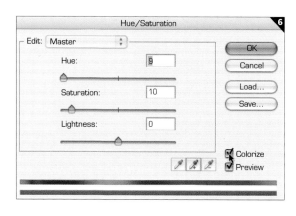

Duotones and Tritones

You may often have wondered how quite a number of the supposedly black and white images that you see in magazines and books look so rich in tone. The answer is that they are not strictly monochrome. In other words, they are not made up purely of different shades of grey.

Because the majority of printers – from those used in professional printing to the vast majority of desktop inkjet or laser printers – are not able accurately to render the subtle changes in tone of a true black and white image, a second, third and even a fourth colour are often added to increase the tonal range, and the print quality. In professional lithographic printers, rollers are used to add colour to an image (usually cyan,

magenta, yellow and black), to make up a full 'four-colour' image. Duotones are created by running the image through a black roller and then another roller with a specified colour, while tritones use a third colour, and quadtones use a fourth.

The additional colours combine with the tones of the true greyscale image, behaving a little like a coloured wash to add whichever colours you wish across the entire image. Photoshop has a powerful set of commands for creating duotones, tritones and quadtones, and these can all sometimes help turn toneless black and white images into much more powerful compositions.

ADDING TONE TO GREYSCALE COMPOSITIONS

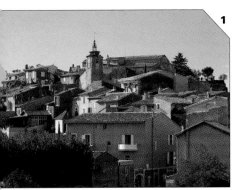

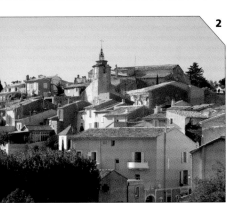

1 Begin with selecting the colour image that you wish to turn into a black and white print. Then, using the conversion technique described on the previous pages, turn the colour photograph into a mono-chrome image.

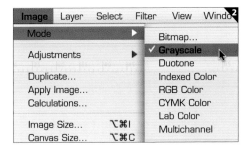

2 After the black and white conversion process is completed, the image looks like it is now monochrome, but it will still have three distinct colour channels (red, green and blue). Before you can continue with the duotone process, you need to delete these channels.

To do this, simply go to Image > Mode > Greyscale. To continue creating the duotone go to Image > Mode > Duotone.

3 Selecting Duotone will bring up the Duotone Options dialog window. If this is the first time you've used the Duotone Options,

Photoshop may introduce a magenta colour as its default, as shown here. This happens because duotones are made up of black and one other colour.

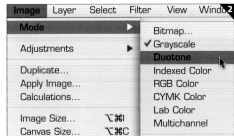

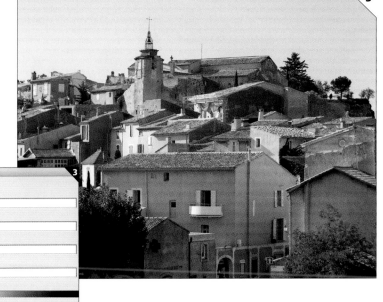

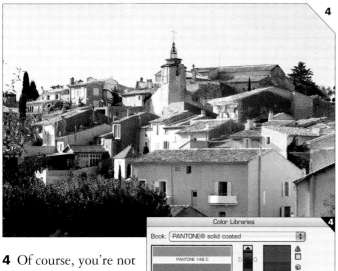

4 Of course, you're not restricted to the default colour if Photoshop has used it. By clicking in the colour square of the second colour, Photoshop brings up the Color Libraries dialog box.

This shows the vast array of colours that is available to you for the creation of the duotone. Here, a light orange colour has been selected to recreate a 'sepia' look.

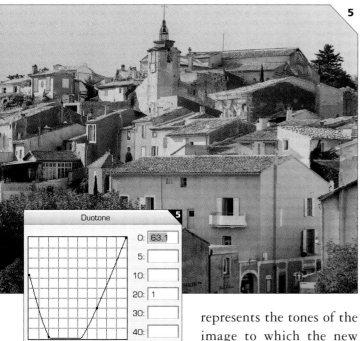

represents the tones of the image to which the new colour will be added.

Here, the point on the left represents the lightest tones in the image, and has been dragged up, resulting in the orange being introduced mainly in the highlight areas. You can alter the curve to help you get a feel for making adjustments.

5 In the Duotone Options window, you'll notice a box next to the colour. Clicking on this box will bring up the Duotone Curve dialog. This looks similar to the Curves dialog box and works in the same way. The straight line

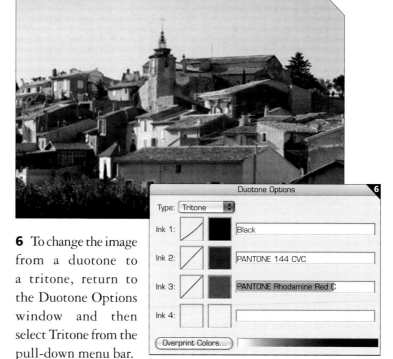

6 To change the image from a duotone to a tritone, return to the Duotone Options window and then select Tritone from the pull-down menu bar.

Click in the colour square to bring up the Color Libraries dialog window to choose a colour for your third 'ink'. In the example shown here, a magenta colour was chosen as the third colour.

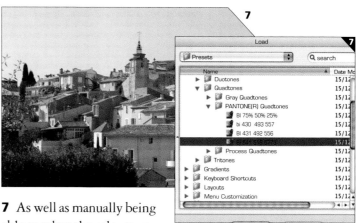

7 As well as manually being able to select the colours you want to use, Photoshop offers a huge array of preset combinations that have been chosen to create a specific atmosphere.

To access the Preset dialog box, click Load in the Duotone Options window. In the Preset window, scroll down to the Duotone folder and open it. The Duotone folder provides a further three folders (Duotone, Tritone and Quadtone), each of which contains numerous preset toning options.

Unfortunately, the names given to the tones aren't particularly descriptive, such as here, where Quadtone Bl 541 513 5773 was used.

When you save your image, you'll only have the option to save it as a Photoshop (.psd) file. This is to ensure that if the file were to go to a professional lithographic printers, they would be able to interpret the settings correctly. However, most inkjet printers are happy printing .psd documents.

Converging Verticals

One of the most common problems with photographs of buildings – particularly extremely tall ones – is that in order to fit the entire building into the frame it's usually necessary to point the camera upward. When you do this, the side walls of the building appear to get closer together the higher up you look. The effect is similar to looking at a long, straight road, where the edges will appear to converge the farther you look down the road. With these long distances, the road often appears to meet at a 'vanishing point', and this is the same with buildings. To achieve really accurate shots of straight buildings, professional photographers use specialist equipment, but you can go some way to improving converging verticals using your image-editing software.

CORRECTING PERSPECTIVE ISSUES

Taken several years ago using a conventional 35mm film camera, this image was then scanned into the computer.

1 This well-exposed picture managed to capture the remarkable detail of the building, so it's worth spending a few minutes on it to adjust the problem of the converging verticals.

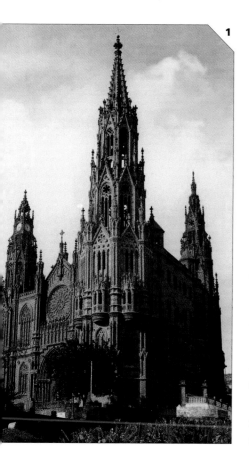

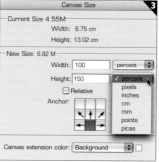

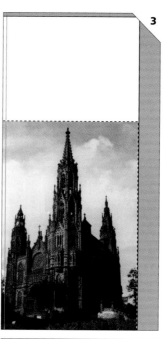

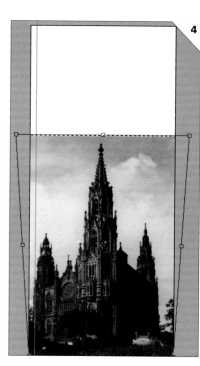

2 Begin by increasing the height of the canvas that you are working on, by going to Image > Canvas Size.

In the dialog window, you should then click the lower middle square next to the Anchor. This indicates that the canvas only needs to be extended upward from the 'ground'.

Click on the pull-down menu next to the height box and select 'percent'. Enter 150 into the height box to increase the height of the canvas by 50%.

3 Using the Rectangular Marquee tool, make a selection of the original image. Next, go to View > Rulers and drag a vertical line from the edge of the frame onto the image area to use as reference to ensure you get the walls vertical.

4 Go to Edit > Transform > Perspective and you will see that corner points appear at the corners as well as at the central points of the sides of the image.

Drag out one corner of the selection and you will notice that the corner point on the opposite side will begin to move out at the same time. Keep dragging until the side walls appear vertical. Compare it with the ruler guide you placed earlier. When it looks as if the vertical walls are

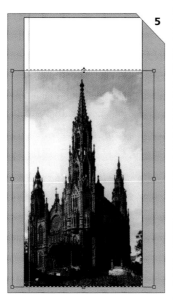

straight, make a note of how much wider the top part of the picture has become by checking the measurements in the Tool Options bar.

Here, the width has been increased by about 120%. Once you're happy with the adjustment, you should confirm by clicking the check box.

5 With the selection still active, go to Image > Transform > Distort. Grab the top middle handle with the cursor and stretch the building upward. The image will stretch in real time, which means you can see the effect of the adjustment as you go.

For guidance, you should keep on stretching the image until the height has reached 120% in order to counter the effect of the perspective adjustment.

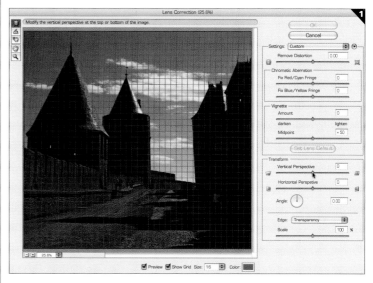

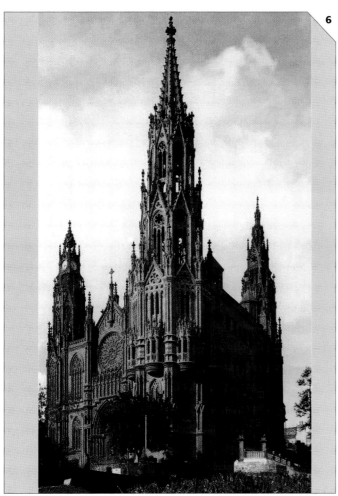

6 To finish, deselect the selection (Select > Deselect) and use the Crop tool to crop out the unused canvas.

USING DISTORTION FILTERS

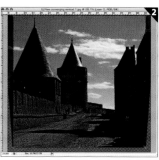

More recent versions of Photoshop and Photoshop Elements have a distortion filter that allows you to correct issues such as converging verticals, as shown here.

1 Go to the Filter menu. In Photoshop it is called Lens Distortion, while in Elements it's known as Correct Camera Distortion; both work in the same way.

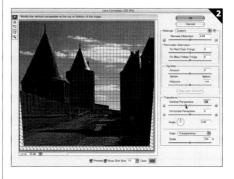

2 By moving the Vertical Perspective slider to the right, the buildings can be set to align with the grid. With the correction made, click OK.

3 Now simply crop away the newly created transparent elements of the image at the bottom of the frame.

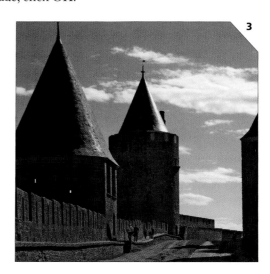

Soft-focus Effect: Landscape

In the days of traditional film cameras, photographers would experiment with numerous materials and techniques to achieve a soft-focus effect, ranging from smearing petroleum jelly on a clear filter fitted to the camera's lens to taking photographs through a pair of old stockings, or simply using a dedicated soft-focus filter.

All of these methods are perfectly valid today, but it's no surprise that it's possible to recreate a soft-focus effect during post-production in almost every image-editing program. Again, this has the benefit that the photographer has greater control over the effect and will also have a straight, unfiltered image.

SOFT FOCUS WITH LAYERS AND FILTERS

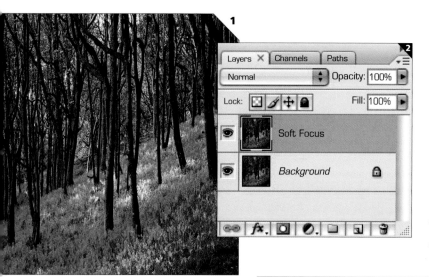

3 Most of the image-editing software packages have a soft-focus filter effect, and Photoshop Elements and the full version of Photoshop are no exception.

In these Adobe programs, the effect is known as Diffuse Glow, and the filter is found under Filter > Distort > Diffuse Glow. There are three sliders that control the overall effect of the filter, and it's well worth spending a little bit of time experimenting with these to see what effect they have on the image in the preview window.

If the image you have is too large for the preview window, you will find that there is a menu at the bottom left-hand corner of the dialog window allowing you to set 'Fit in View'.

1 This striking image of a field of spring bluebells in a wood is exactly the sort of photograph that might be successfully enhanced by incorporating filters and layers for a soft-focus effect.

2 Start by duplicating the Background layer (Layer > Duplicate layer), so you can delete any effects that you don't want, while retaining the original.

An alternative method of duplicating the layer is to go to the Layers palette and then drag the Background image thumbnail onto the 'Create a new layer' icon. It's helpful to rename the new layer 'Soft focus'.

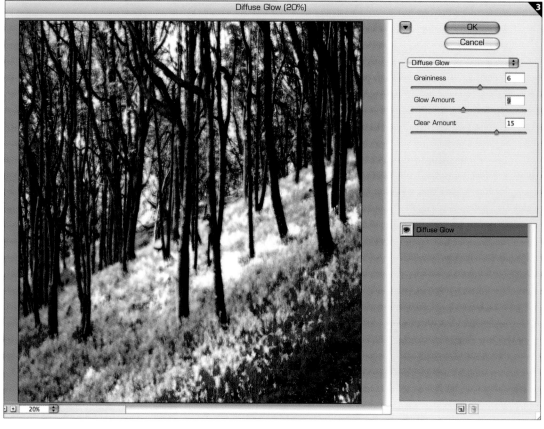

4 Once you feel happy with the filter effect in the preview window, click OK, and the filter will then be applied to the copy of the original image. The Diffuse Glow filter in Photoshop has created a pleasing effect, but you may decide that you want to reintroduce some of the original colour of the bluebells by reducing the Opacity of the Soft-focus layer in the Layers palette.

5 If your software doesn't have a soft-focus filter, or if you're not pleased with the result the filter provides, the alternative is to use Gaussian blur instead.

On the Soft-focus layer apply a fairly liberal amount of Gaussian blur. Here, the Radius has been set to 30 to give an obvious soft-focus feel to the image.

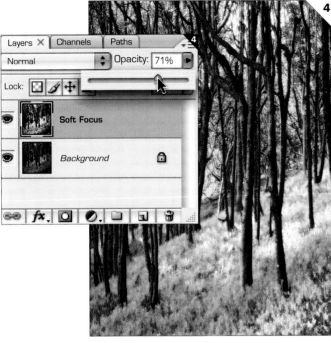

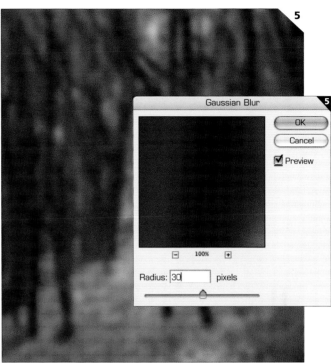

6 As well as blurring the duplicate layer, it's worth brightening it using Levels (Image > Adjustments > Levels). Here, the white and central gamma points have both been moved to the left.

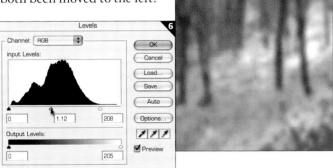

7 Return to the Layers palette and reduce the Soft-focus layer's Opacity so that the original image begins to show through, as before.

At this point, you should try experimenting with the Opacity slider until you've reached the right amount of softening, then go to Layer > Flatten Image to combine the layers. It's worth remembering that once the layers have been flattened, you'll need to give the file a separate name or you'll overwrite the original. To do this, go to Save As and then key in an appropriate name.

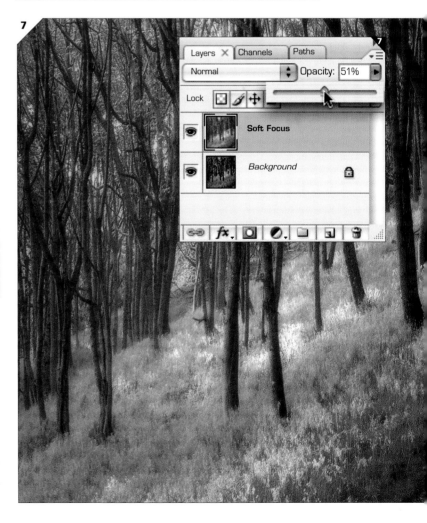

Soft-focus Effect: Portrait

It's not just landscapes that can benefit from a soft-focus treatment. For many years, portrait photographers who shot on film also used soft-focus techniques and effects in their work. Often, soft-focus filters were used to flatter the sitter, as the softening effect hides blemishes and can make skin appear smoother. Alternatively, the effect could be used to provide a more dreamy, other-worldly result, which particularly suits portraits of children. The digital technique for a soft-focus portrait is quite similar to that of the soft-focus landscape, but it involves the use of Blending Modes, and introduces one or two further steps to fine-tune the result.

SOFT FOCUS USING BLENDING MODES

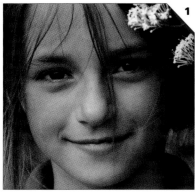

1 Here, we're going to apply a digital soft-focus effect to this portrait using Photoshop. Of course, the same technique can be used in other editing software. Although the girl is young enough to show no signs of ageing, the effect will give the shot additional charm.

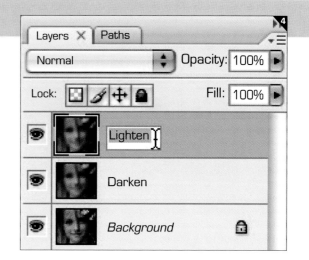

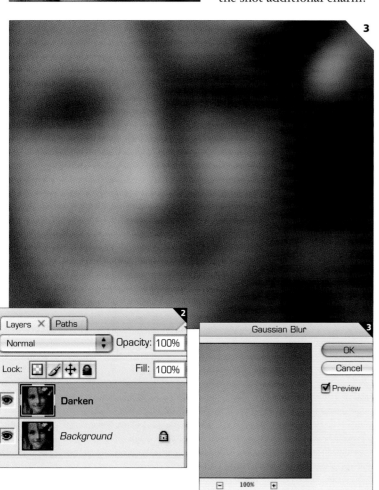

2 Begin by duplicating the Background layer. You can do this either in the Layers palette by dragging the Background thumbnail onto the 'Create a new layer' icon or by going to Layer > Duplicate layer.

As before, it is a good idea to rename the new layer, in this case 'Darken', as this helps you to keep track of the various layers as you work through the project.

3 As with the soft-focus landscape effect, go to the Filter menu and select Blur > Gaussian Blur.

Set a large Radius of around 30 pixels. As you have seen with the landscape project, the image will become instantly indistinct and unrecognizable.

4 Duplicate the Darken layer using the same method as duplicating the Background layer described in Step 2. Rename this third layer 'Lighten'.

Click on the Darken layer and, using the drop-down menu at the top of the Layers palette, select the Darken blending mode. Next, reduce the Opacity to around 40% but note that this will have no visible effect on the image at this stage.

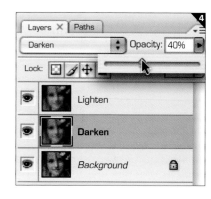

5 Next, click on the Lighten layer and set the Blending Mode to Lighten. Reduce the Opacity to around 60%.

At this stage, the soft-focus effect should have become apparent. However, by applying it to the entire portrait, the sparkle in the eyes, which is one of the most important elements of a portrait, has been lost.

6 To bring back some of the missing spark, we need to reduce the effect of the soft-focus 'filter'.

To do this, select the Darken layer and click on the 'Add Layer mask' icon at the bottom of the Layers palette. This will introduce a new blank Layer mask thumbnail next to the Darken layer thumbnail.

7 First, ensure that the Layer mask is active (it will be framed by a thin black border if it is) before going to the Toolbox to choose the Brush tool. With black as the foreground colour, start painting over the eyes.

Remember that you can easily adjust the size of the brush using the '[' and ']' keys. As you paint over the portrait, the eyes should come back into focus and regain their sparkle. Notice how the Layer mask in the Layers palette will also indicate which areas you have been painting.

If you want to return to a more soft-focus effect, just press 'X' to change the foreground colour to white and paint the mask back in.

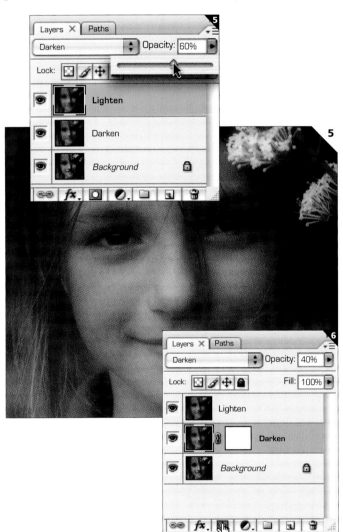

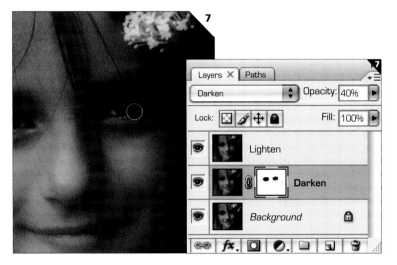

8 When you have finished, the final photograph ought to appear as a pleasing soft-focus portrait that has softened the main facial features and the skin, but which still enables the eyes to show clearly through. Once you're fully satisfied with the final result, you need to go to Layer > Flatten Image and save.

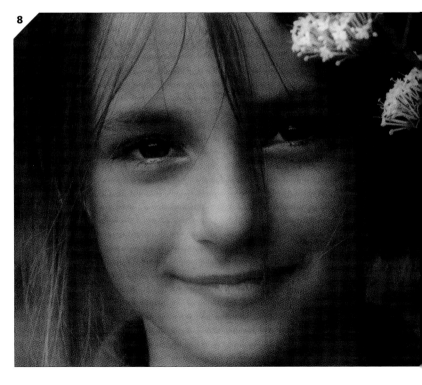

Soft-focus alternative

The technique described here uses Layer masks, which are not available in some image-editing packages, such as Photoshop Elements.

However, a very similar effect can be achieved by simply duplicating the Background layer and applying the Gaussian Blur filter to the new layer. You need to reduce the Opacity of the blurred layer in the Layers palette and then use the Eraser tool to reveal the sharper background layer.

Recreating Depth of Field

Depth of field is one of the indispensable tools of the creative photographer. For stunning landscapes, setting a narrow aperture, compensated for by a long exposure, can help achieve pin-sharp focus on everything from the closest foreground detail to the horizon.

But when shooting portraits, sports, children or food, using a wide aperture to reduce the depth of field can add impact and drama. Because limiting the depth of field

in this way demands a reasonably fast (and expensive) lens, it's also one of the factors that differentiates professional shots from the average holiday snap. If it proves impracticable to shoot with a wide aperture to get a shallow depth of field, or you just don't think of it until you're looking at the finished image, the effect can be recreated using software, with the careful application of selective blurring. The challenge is to make it look real.

APPLYING A SHALLOW DEPTH OF FIELD

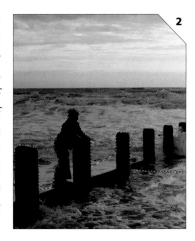

1 First, decide where you want the point of focus of the image to be. Usually, your intention will be to bring out a particular object or figure. In this photograph, it's the boy standing on the groyne.

You'll need to make a selection to separate this from the rest of the scene, using one of the methods shown earlier. The selection doesn't need to be absolutely precise for this technique, so you can work quickly.

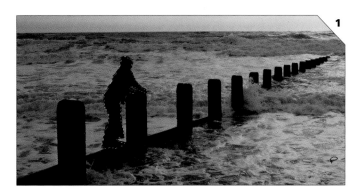

2 Creating a depth of field effect that's realistic isn't as simple as keeping your intended subject sharp and blurring the rest of the scene. Everything of equal distance from the lens should seem equally sharp, so you need to add anything that lies on the same focal plane as your initial subject.

In this picture, nothing is directly in line with the figure except the groyne, so the Rectangular Marquee tool can be used to select the strip of groyne around the boy.

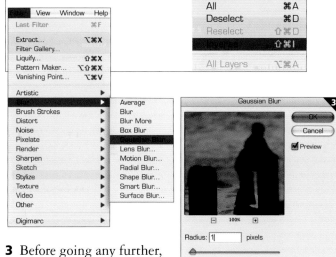

3 Before going any further, you should save your selection by choosing Select > Save Selection. Remember to select 'New' at the top, give your selection a name, and then click OK so that it is saved for future reference.

What you actually want to select now is the area that you're going to blur, which means everything outside your subject. Choose Select >Inverse to invert the selection. You may also want to hide the 'marching ants' border temporarily by pressing Ctrl + H (on a PC) or Command + H (on a Mac). Then, once you have done this, go to Filter >

Blur > Gaussian Blur. In the Gaussian Blur dialog box, the Radius setting governs the strength of the blurring. To create the impression of depth of field, you will require a Radius of several pixels.

If you attempt this in one go, you'll find that it will create an unnatural halo effect around the subject, which will even be visible in the preview.

Here, for instance, you can see that the colours within the subject appear to be 'leaking out' into the background.

4 To avoid this, start with just a 1 pixel blur Radius. Click OK, then go to Select > Modify > Contract.

In the dialog box, set a size of 3 pixels and click OK. This will make the selection shrink away from the subject. However, since the selection no longer follows the outline of an object, you'll need to feather it to avoid the problem of creating a hard edge, so go to Select > Feather. Set a Radius of 3 pixels and click OK. Having done this, reopen Gaussian Blur and this time set Radius to 1.5 pixels. Click OK.

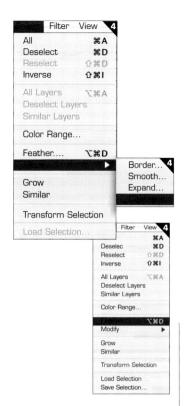

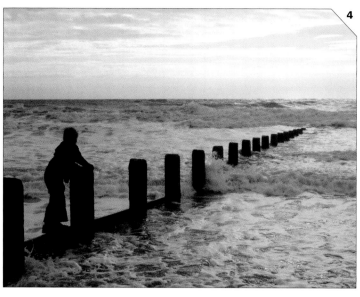

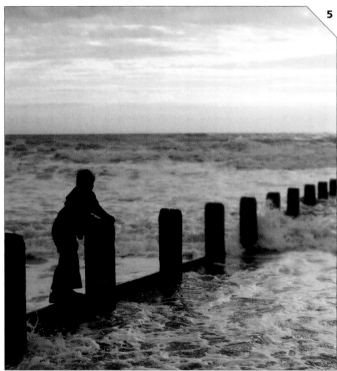

5 To complete the depth of field effect, you just need to repeat the same sequence of three filters with slightly larger sizes each time: for example, 10 pixels for Contract and Feather, and 10 pixels for Gaussian Blur, then going to 40 pixels and so on. In most scenes, these steps will give a realistic result without forcing you to think about where the focus should fall off. Here the sea in the background ends up looking heavily blurred. It is also the area that would be most out of focus if you took the shot using a wide aperture.

The resulting image is a believable narrow depth of field shot, with the emphasis on the figure.

QUICK FIX USING LAYER MASK

Using layer masks, you can emulate depth of field.

1 Duplicating the background layer, click Add layer mask. Next, draw a Black to Transparent gradient over the image once the mask is active. The areas painted black will stay in focus.

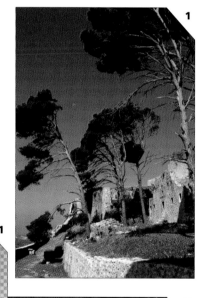

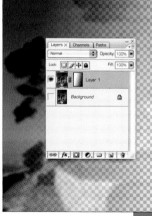

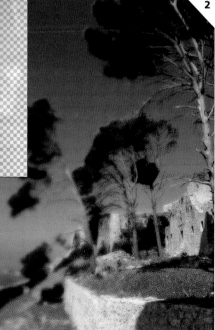

2 On the duplicate layer, click on the thumbnail and apply Gaussian Blur. The gradually un-masked area will become blurred leaving the masked area sharp.

Creating Panoramas

The concept of taking a number of consecutive images along the length of the same scene in order to stitch them together to create one long panorama has been around for a long while now. Today, increasing numbers of digital camera manufacturers are going to great lengths to develop dedicated 'Panorama' settings for their cameras, which allow photographers to align the individual shots more accurately.

Image-editing software manufacturers have constantly refined their applications to improve the stitching capabilities of the programs. Adobe's latest version of Photoshop, for example, is now so sophisticated that it's no longer necessary to use a tripod and manual exposure to ensure an accurate end result – the software will deal with this for you. But if you don't have such advanced software, here's the best way to achieve great results.

STITCHING TOGETHER A SET OF IMAGES

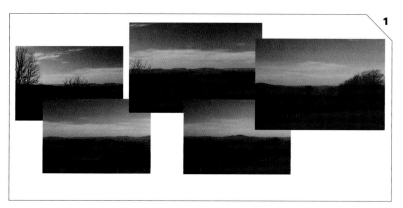

3 In this specific case, you can see that even the mighty Photoshop CS2 hasn't done a particularly good job of aligning the images. So, you will need to make changes to the image manually.

4 By clicking on parts of the image, the pictures can be rearranged into the correct order. Photoshop will then automatically align the images by matching the pixels together.

1 These five images were taken using a tripod and, having determined an acceptable exposure for the entire scene, they were all shot in manual mode. The tripod helps you to align the various images accurately, while shooting in manual ensures there's no variation in the brightness values of the individual shots.

Once the shots have been taken, download them, and place them in a folder on your computer's hard drive for safety.

2 To start, bring up the Photomerge dialog box in Photoshop, and go to File > Automate > Photomerge.

Navigate to the files that you have decided to include in the panorama and then click OK.

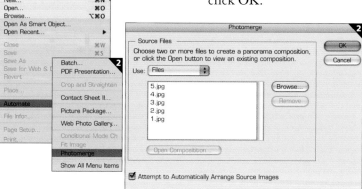

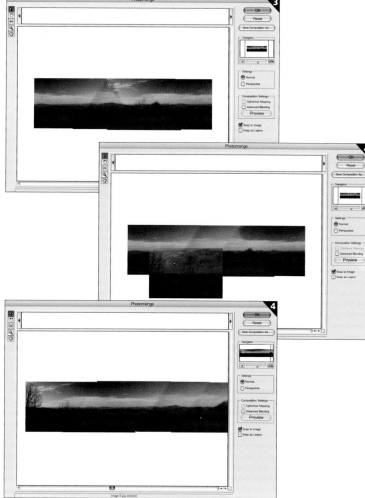

5 With the shots now in the correct order, selecting Advanced Blending will greatly improve the 'joins' between the images, as shown in the Preview.

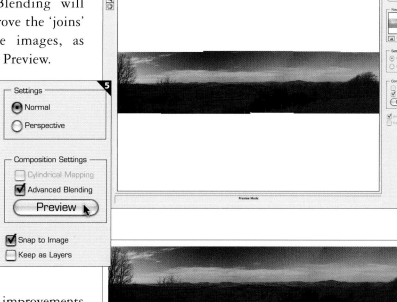

6 Before any improvements are made to this panorama, you need to cut away any of the landscape's unwanted background area using the Crop tool. This will also help to keep the file size to a minimum.

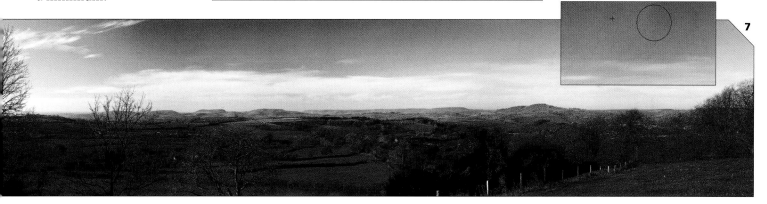

7 With the background cut away, perform any global changes you'd like to make to the panorama. Here, for example, the brightness has been increased using the Levels command.

Now zoom in to fix specific areas in the image that don't match exactly. With so much sky in this image, some of the tones aren't equal. Use the Clone Stamp tool to correct these, along with any areas where the join is visible.

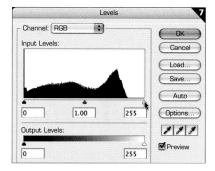

8 Photoshop CS3 and Elements 6 have a more powerful picture-stitching tool, which works in much the same way as in previous versions, but when you open Photomerge you have various options for stitching the images together. The 'Panorama' setting offers a true panorama representation, while the 'Cylindrical' setting will provide the view that we're more accustomed to, as does 'Reposition Only'.

It does pay to experiment with these various options. However, note how CS3 and Elements have both merged the images so successfully that, in fact, no remedial work (other than tone and colour) has been required to get to the finished image.

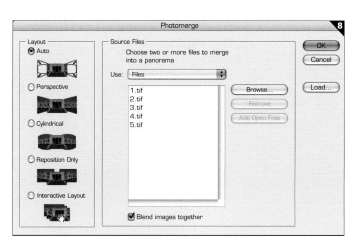

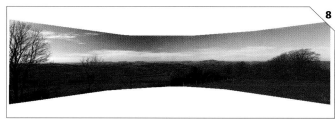

Hand-tinted Photographs

Before the advent of colour photography, the only way to add colour to a photograph was to use coloured oil paints and physically paint the image.

Although the results were never intended to be realistic in the way we view colour pictures today, hand-tinted photographs were immensely popular and they achieved a unique visual quality that couldn't be replicated with the arrival of colour film.

With image-editing software, it's now possible to recreate the effect of 'vintage' hand-tinted photographs, but without the mess – or irreversible nature – of paint. The exercise is easy and fun, and an ideal project for children. The colours can be as muted or as garish as you like, and can either emulate the look of old, Victorian, hand-tinted photographs or can create vibrant works that appear to be influenced by modern artists.

ADDING COLOUR TO A COLOUR IMAGE

In this first example, the starting point for adding colour is a colour image.

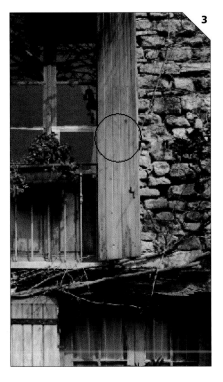

1 In the Layers palette, duplicate the Background layer by dragging the thumbnail onto the 'Create a new layer' icon, or by going to Layer > Duplicate Layer.

2 Select the duplicate layer, go to Image > Adjustments > Desaturate and create a black and white image.

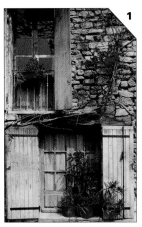

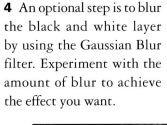

3 All you need to do now is select the Eraser tool from the Toolbox and then set the Opacity in the Tool Options bar to between 30% and 40%.

Next, simply erase the black and white image to reveal the colour layer that is underneath.

4 An optional step is to blur the black and white layer by using the Gaussian Blur filter. Experiment with the amount of blur to achieve the effect you want.

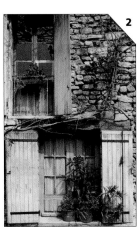

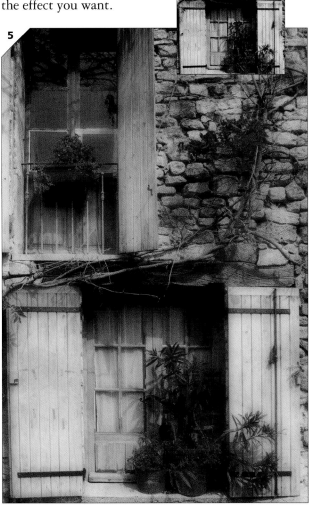

5 As always, you can adjust the Opacity of the top layer to increase or reduce the intensity of the colour.

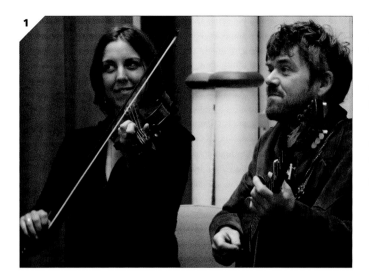

Here, the black and white image could have been scanned into the computer, shot in black and white mode on a digital camera, or converted to black and white.

1 Begin the exercise for this image by going to Image > Mode > RGB Color, so that you can add colour to the image.

2 Next, we need to duplicate the Background layer (Layer > Duplicate layer). In the Layers palette, change the duplicate layer's Blending Mode to Color using the drop-down menu. Then, make sure that you rename the layer 'Colour'.

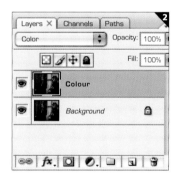

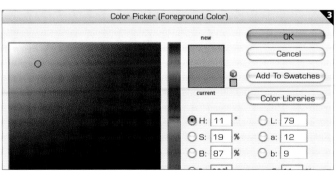

3 The first tone you need to add is a flesh tone to all the exposed areas of skin. One option for doing this is to open a colour image that features a flesh tone (such as a portrait), and then use the Eyedropper tool to sample an appropriate area. Click on the skin to change the foreground colour to the chosen tone. This will be visible in the Foreground Color box at the bottom of the Toolbox.

Alternatively, you can click on the Foreground Color box to bring up the Color Picker. Navigate your way to an appropriate colour by using the slider and the cursor.

4 Choose a small, soft brush (adjustable with the '[' and ']' keys) and set an Opacity of around 30% in the Tool Options bar.

Start to paint over areas of skin on the Colour layer with the flesh tone you selected in Step 3.

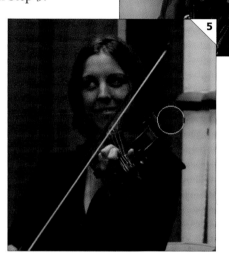

5 Once you've coloured the skin, return to the Color Picker and choose colours for other areas of the image. Don't worry too much about painstakingly painting in the exact areas, as the intention is to create only the suggestion of colour for each major element of the image, rather than to create a full-colour photograph.

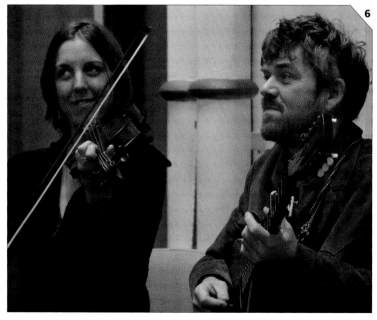

6 For this image, a total of six colours were used to colour the entire photograph. The Colour layer was then blurred slightly using the Gaussian Blur filter.

Restoring Old Photographs

The various cloning options and healing brushes covered earlier in this book are extremely powerful and versatile tools, and are ideal for fixing and restoring old or damaged photographs. These are a significant advance on the conventional restoration methods using inks and tiny paintbrushes that were all that was available several years ago. Nowadays, armed just with a desktop scanner, a computer and some fairly inexpensive image-editing software, it's possible to repair photographs to a much higher standard.

USING SOFTWARE TO RESTORE IMAGES

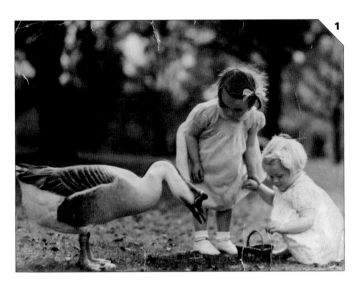

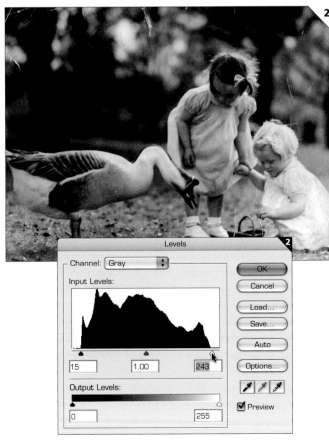

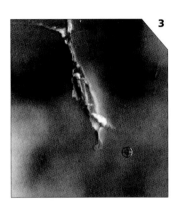

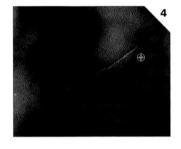

1 This delightful picture of two sisters feeding a Chinese goose was taken in 1938. The last 70 years haven't been kind to the original print and there are tears, creases and numerous dust and scratch marks.

2 After scanning the print, the first step is to check the tonal levels. Opening the Levels dialog (Image > Adjustments > Levels) shows that both the black and white points aren't at their optimum. Both points have been brought in a little so they sit under the ends of the histogram, giving the image a little more contrast.

3 The next step is to systematically fix and restore the numerous tears, creases and scratches. For large damaged areas, the best tool is likely to be the Clone Stamp tool. Clone a point that matches as closely as possible the area you're trying to repair, and remember to keep taking samples from other areas to avoid creating repeating patterns. Remember to use the '[' and ']' keys to choose a brush of the appropriate size. Use Edit > Undo to reverse any corrections that go slightly wrong.

4 For much smaller scratches, try using the Healing Brush tool. Sample as closely as you can to the area to be repaired and move slowly along the scratch.

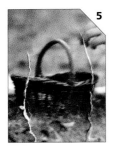 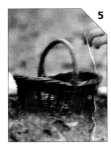 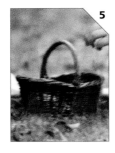 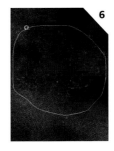 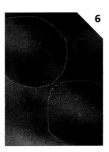 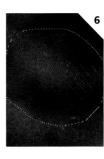

5 All images will have slightly more complex areas to repair. For these, you should revert to the Clone Stamp tool and then sample those areas that share the same pattern as those you are attempting to repair. It's possible that you may find suitable sampling points in entirely different parts of the scene.

6 If you have the option of using a Patch tool, try using this on those areas where there is no obvious pattern, such as here, where the emulsion has become rather sticky, leaving a drying mark. Now draw around the offending area and drag it to an area that closely resembles the part that you are trying to correct.

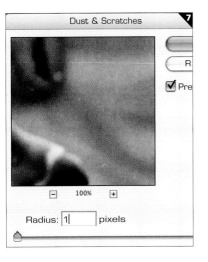

7 This particular image was also suffering from a fair amount of dust damage.

To remedy this, apply the Dust & Scratches filter (Filter > Noise > Dust & Scratches), with a very small Radius. Too high a Radius will often soften an image to an unacceptable level.

8 Having made the repairs, the image should almost be as good as the original.

9 With the image stored in your computer, you can make any number of changes to it. Here, Hue/Saturation was used, clicking the Colorize option to apply a light sepia tone. With a Levels adjustment layer, the contrast was then increased to give the picture a vintage feel.

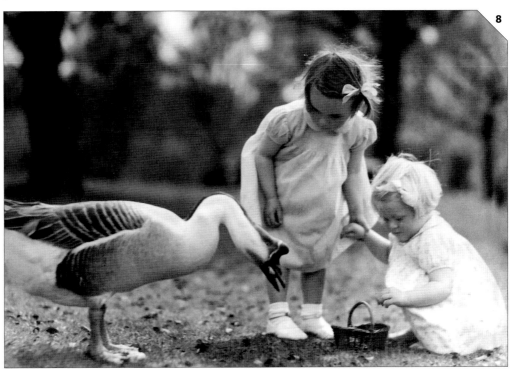

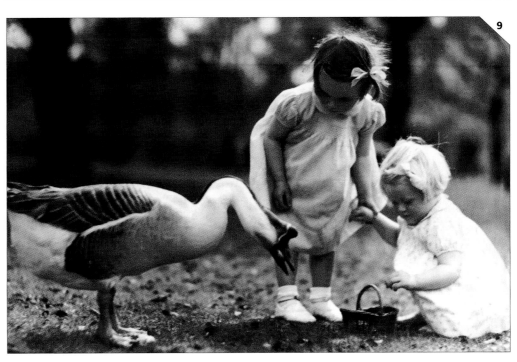

Retouching Portaits

The great thing about digital images is that they can be easily altered, right down to the pixel level if necessary. This means that it's not only really easy to fix old and damaged photographs once they've been scanned, but it is also easy to edit and fix less-than-perfect digital shots.

One of the most common retouching techniques is to remove skin blemishes and the subtle signs of age in portrait pictures. Practically every image you see in advertising (particularly in the fashion and beauty industry) has been 'fixed' digitally to make the models appear as perfect as possible.

However, it's quite straightforward to do similar work yourself using image-editing software. Without going to quite the extremes that the fashion industry does, impressive results can be achieved relatively quickly and easily using a few simple commands and common tools.

DIGITALLY RETOUCHING SKIN

1 The subject in this shot has a few wrinkles, crow's feet around the eyes, and the odd blemish here and there – a bit like most of us. Using almost any editing software, the age lines can be reduced and the skin generally cleaned up to make the subject appear younger.

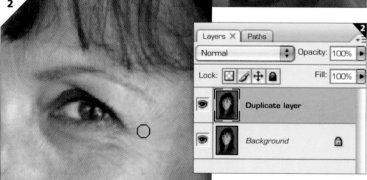

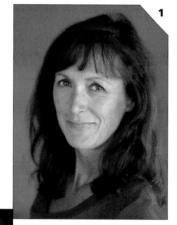

2 Close inspection shows the task at hand in more detail. The first step is to remove (or reduce) the crow's feet around the left eye.

First, make a duplicate copy of the Background layer before you start working. By doing this, you can easily rectify any mistakes, or reduce slightly over-zealous retouching. Preserving the original also makes it quick and easy to make before-and-after comparisons.

Using the Clone Stamp tool and a small, soft brush set to an Opacity of around 40% in the Tool Options bar, sample an area close to the uppermost line of the left eye's crow's feet and simply clone it out in one smooth stroke. As you work down you'll have more clean skin to sample.

3 The laughter lines around the subject's mouth can also be removed or at least smoothed out slightly, but for this adjustment it's far better to use a larger brush because the skin tone changes quite a bit.

The larger radius and soft edge of the brush will help even out the variation in tone and therefore ensure that the image retains a realistic appearance.

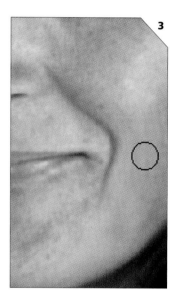

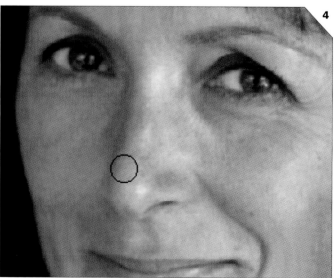

4 Once all the major lines have been removed on both sides of the face and on the forehead, you can start fixing the blemishes on the nose. Sample areas of similarly coloured skin with the Clone Stamp tool and dab out the marks.

5 Finally, create a new layer by clicking on the 'Create a new layer' icon in the Layers palette.

Using the Eyedropper tool to take samples, paint over the duplicated original with the Brush tool, making sure you concentrate on areas where you want to even up the skin colour. Applied carefully, and with a low Opacity set in the Tool options bar, this will add the final gloss to the end result.

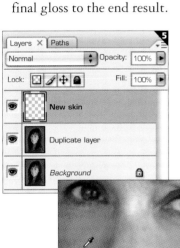

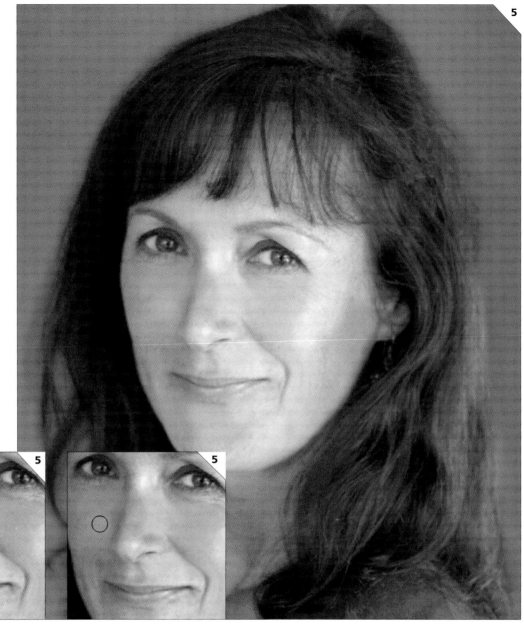

QUICK RETOUCHING WITH GAUSSIAN BLUR

For a very quick fix, you can use the same technique for soft-focus portrait effect, but to a lesser degree.

1 Duplicate the background image, then apply a small amount of Gaussian Blur (you can experiment with quantity).

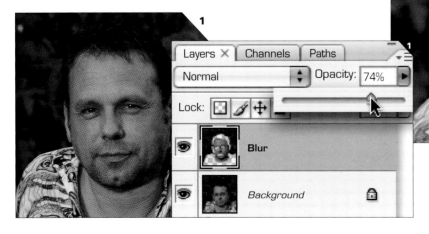

2 Next, use the Eraser tool to erase the blurred layer around the eyes, mouth, hair and any other areas you would like to remain sharp.

Adding Type

Having the ability to create type for use on its own or to add to images allows the amateur photographer to turn into an amateur graphic designer, albeit for a short period of time. Adding type to images opens up a whole new world of possibilities, ranging from greeting cards and invitations, through to postcards and CD cover designs. The possibilities are literally endless.

Just about all image-editing applications have some form of type capability, but some are more sophisticated than others. Photoshop and Photoshop Elements have plenty to offer, and adding type to an image using either package is easy and intuitive. The range of type fonts, styles and effects is breathtaking – and it's possible to download even more fonts from the Internet.

INTRODUCING TEXT TO IMAGES

1 To begin adding text to an image, select the Text tool from the Toolbox. Photoshop, Elements and many other image-editing programs feature both Horizontal and Vertical Text tools. Here, the Horizontal type tool has been chosen.

With the Text tool now selected, place the cursor in the approximate position that you want the text to appear. Don't worry too much at this stage about getting it in exactly the right place, as you can move the text at any time until you flatten the image's layers.

2 Type the text you want to appear. The type will appear in the style of the last font that you used.

Once you've finished typing, click OK in the Tool Options bar. When you press OK, a new layer with your text is automatically created in the Layers palette.

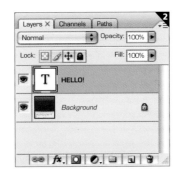

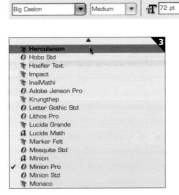

3 Once you've placed the text on the image, you can then style it in any number of ways. Going to the Tool Options bar presents you with the opportunity to select or change the type font, size and colour. There are a huge number of fonts to choose from, and usually one that will serve your purpose.

4 Clicking on the 'Create warped text' icon brings up the Warp Text dialog. This features numerous weird and wacky custom shapes and patterns that allow you to shape your words. Clicking on a specific shape, such as 'Fisheye', brings up a further dialog box where you can control the specific size and shape of the effect.

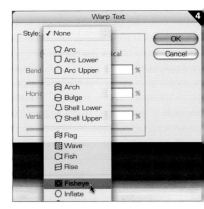

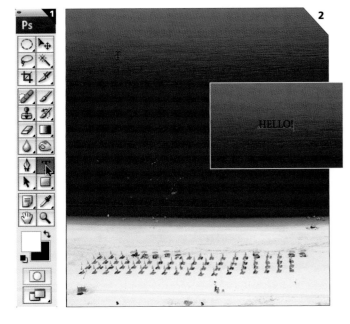

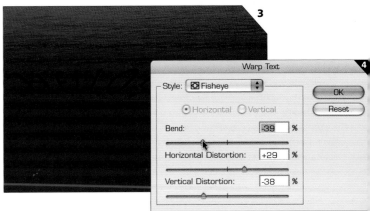

5 Once you've selected the Warp Text style, go to the Layers palette and click on the 'Create layer style' icon. This will bring up a whole host of additional styles that can be applied to your type.

Here, 'Drop Shadow' has been selected. 'Outer Glow' was then selected in the Layer Style dialog box and some adjustments to the 'Drop Shadow' settings were made to achieve the effect shown here.

6 The black type looks a little dull, but clicking on the coloured box in the Tool Options bar brings up the Color Picker, where you can quickly and easily select a different colour.

Having chosen a colour and applied Layer styles to the text layer, return to the Layers palette and then you can see precisely which styles have been applied.

Clicking on any of the style icons will bring up the relevant dialog box where further adjustments can then be made.

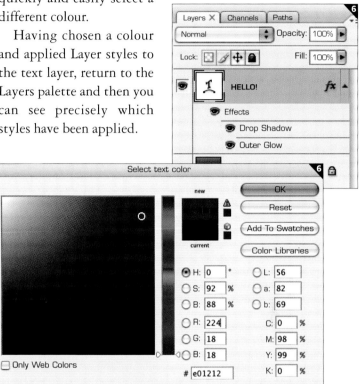

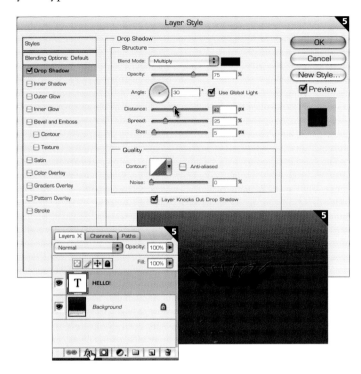

7 Finally, before 'fixing' the type, click on the Move tool and, with 'Show Bounding Box' checked in the Tool Options bar, you can now reposition, rotate and stretch your text.

8 Clicking on the Type tool to add additional text will keep on creating new layers that you can refine, style and re-edit until you eventually decide to go to Layer > Flatten Layers.

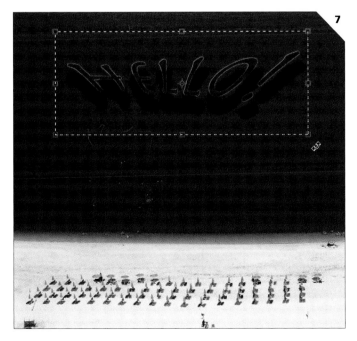

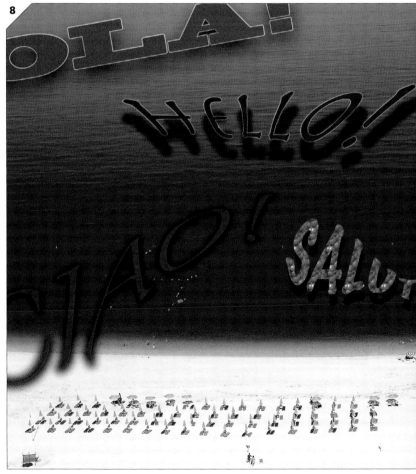

Adding Borders

Having created your own photographic masterpiece, why not try adding a border as a final creative touch? As with just about anything related to image-editing, there are countless ways of adding a border to an image, but the method described here allows you to experiment freely and easily with Adobe's extensive and powerful set of

Filters, available in both Elements and Photoshop. Other programs have similar filter sets that can be applied in the same way, and if you don't like the one you initially select you can go back and try another until you find one you do like. Sooner or later you'll find a border effect that adds a touch of professionalism to your image.

USING A FILTER TO ADD A BORDER

1 Open the image to which you want to add a border, then select the Rectangular Marquee tool and draw a border around the inside edge of the image. You could just as easily use the Elliptical Marquee tool to create an oval border around the image, or you could even draw a freehand border with the Lasso tool.

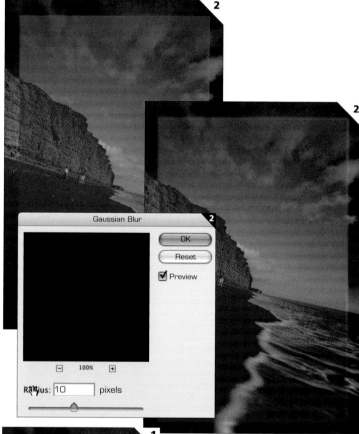

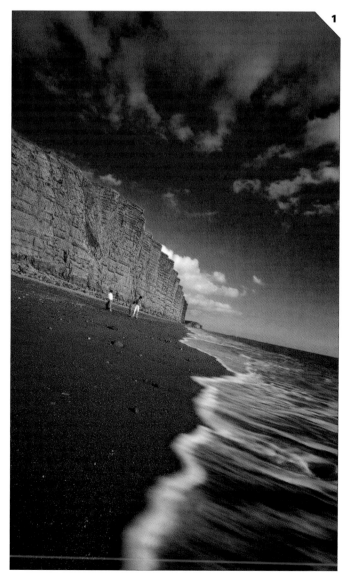

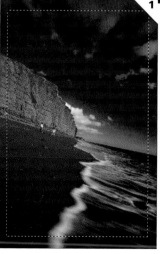

2 With the border in place, go to Select > Inverse and then click the 'Edit in quick mask mode' icon at the bottom of the Toolbox. Blur the mask slightly using Gaussian Blur (Filter > Blur > Gaussian Blur). The more blur you add at this stage, the more noticeable the blur will become when you get to the end.

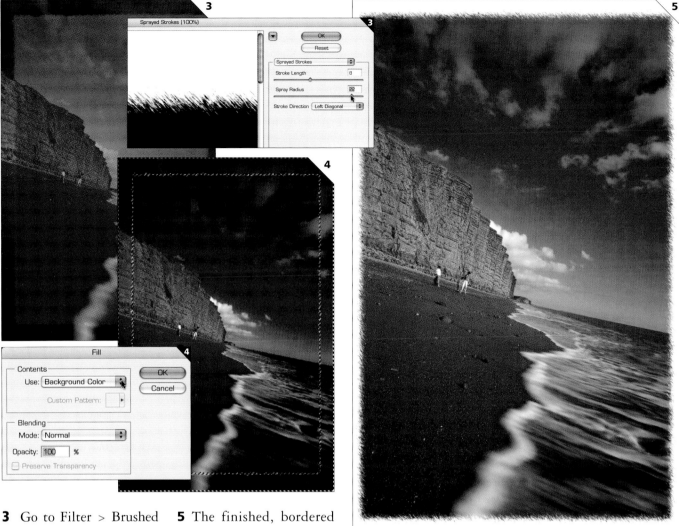

3 Go to Filter > Brushed Strokes > Sprayed Strokes, and experiment with the settings until you see a result you like in the preview window. You should remember that you are applying this filter to the mask, rather than the image itself, and bear in mind that the higher the resolution of the image, the less the effect of the filter. When you're happy with the settings, click OK.

4 To return to the main image, click the Quick Mask mode icon to turn the mask into a 'marching ants' selection. Then go to Edit > Fill and fill the border with a colour you feel is appropriate. In this example, white was chosen as the border colour.

5 The finished, bordered image is shown here.

ALTERNATIVE BORDERS

In the additional examples shown here, the same technique has been used to apply borders using the Extrude Edges, Glass (Tiny Lens), and Spatter filters. Experiment using any filter you like; some, however, are more appropriate for this task than others. You can use the History palette to go back each time to try another option – just delete the Filter Gallery line and start again with another filter. If you don't find a filter that works for your image, numerous websites allow you to view and download other border effects – some you have to pay for, but others are free.

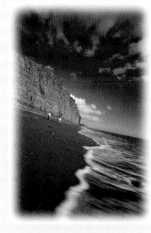

Spatter

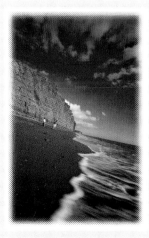

Glass (Tiny Lens)

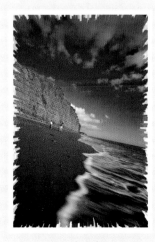

Extrude Edges

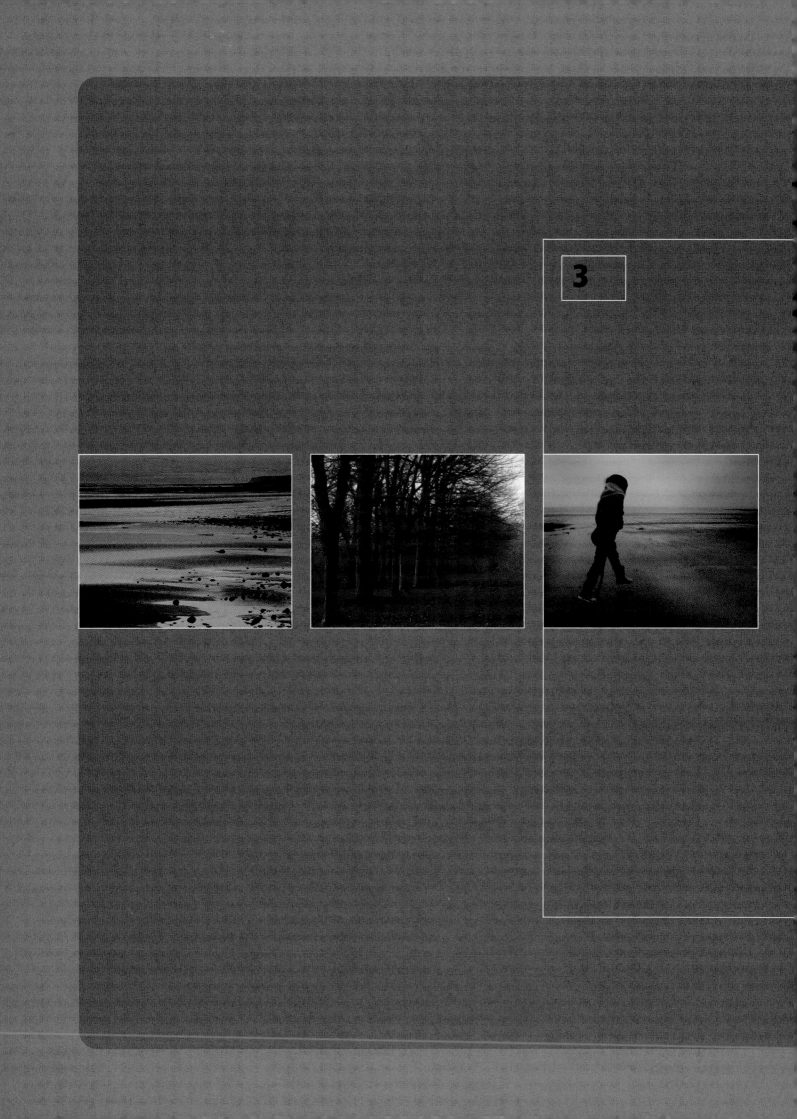

3

Viewing and Sharing

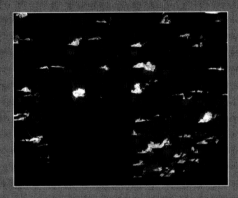 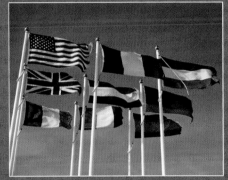 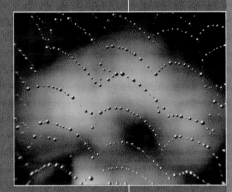

Whether it's simple family snaps or potential competition-winning art photographs, sooner or later you'll either want to make prints or create an electronic version that can be sent via e-mail, or create a slideshow on disk. Chapter 3 provides you with all the information you need to produce professional-looking prints, or to choose a series of images that you can then transform into a picture gallery or slideshow, complete with captions and background soundtrack. There is also plenty of useful information on the different types of printers available, and how to produce the best prints at home.

Scanners and Scanning

While most amateur photographers and more and more professionals now shoot exclusively with digital cameras, many people still find a scanner a useful addition to their digital photography workflow. You may have a number of old prints, negatives or slides you would like to work on digitally, which can be edited and enhanced in some way, or you might still prefer shooting using high-resolution, medium-format film that then needs to be scanned before printing. There could be any number of reasons for wanting the ability to scan images into the computer.

Flatbed or film

There are two types of desktop scanner – flatbed and film. The former is the most common, featuring a hinged lid that closes down over a glass surface, or 'platen'. The size of the platen determines the size of the prints that can be scanned. Most flatbed scanners are A4 paper size, capable of scanning prints up to around 10 x 8in (25 x 20cm), which is more than enough for most needs. Most recent flatbed models also feature some form of film

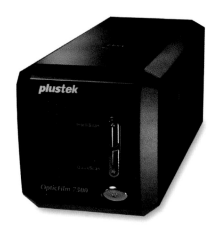

ABOVE If you still shoot a lot of film or have a large library of film images, a film scanner will provide you with the necessary resolution to capture all the detail from the film.

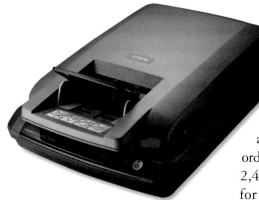

ABOVE Most flatbed scanners have a built-in transparency hood, which means you can scan your slides and negatives, as well as prints.

or slide carrier in the lid, known as a transparency hood, making it possible to scan individual slides or strips of film. However, flatbed scanners are primarily designed to scan prints, and many do not offer the high resolution needed to make the most of film. For this reason, if most of the material you intend to scan is film, you'll get better results from a dedicated film scanner.

What to look for

Both film and flatbed scanners work in more or less the same way. An imaging sensor, such as a CCD, records the colour and tonal information from the print or film, which is converted and stored as digital data in much the same way as it is in a digital camera. The difference is that the sensor in a scanner scans the information a line at a time, hence the term 'scanner'.

Resolution

There are three factors to bear in mind when looking to buy a scanner: resolution, colour depth and dynamic range. Resolution figures for scanners are often given as two figures, such as 2,400 x 4,800ppi. The first figure represents the actual 'optical' scanning resolution of the sensor, while the second represents how

finely the scanner head moves. Rely on the first figure and ensure the figure you're quoted is the actual resolution and not an 'interpolated' one. If you want a flatbed scanner to scan images in order to make prints, a resolution of 2,400ppi will be perfectly adequate for most uses. For film scanners, a higher resolution is required, and around 4,800ppi would be sufficient.

Colour depth

The number of colours a device is capable of recognizing is also key. Even the most basic scanners offer 24-bit colour, meaning they are able to distinguish among 16.7 million colours. If you can afford to, buy a scanner that offers 36-, 42- or even 48-bit colour. The increased colour depth will provide you with greater scope when editing the colour in your images, as well as being able to better render detail in shadow areas.

Dynamic range

Another factor governing a scanner's ability to capture subtle detail in highlights and shadows is its dynamic range. Dynamic range in scanners runs on a scale with a theoretical maximum of 4.8. In reality, professional drum scanners with a resolution of 11,000ppi achieve a figure of around 4. For flatbed scanners, you should look for a model with a dynamic range (DMax) of 3+ if you are scanning colour prints. For scanning film, look for a dynamic range of 3.8+.

Be wary of manufacturers' claims, as there is no standard means of measuring dynamic range, so two scanners with the same quoted DMax figure might not actually have the same dynamic range.

Scanning

All scanners come equipped with their own software that enables them to perform scans. Once this software is loaded onto the computer you can either start scanning by launching the newly loaded software, or you can usually access the software via your image-editing software.

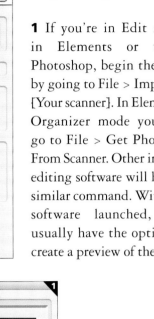

1 If you're in Edit mode in Elements or using Photoshop, begin the scan by going to File > Import > [Your scanner]. In Elements' Organizer mode you can go to File > Get Photos > From Scanner. Other image-editing software will have a similar command. With the software launched, you usually have the option to create a preview of the scan.

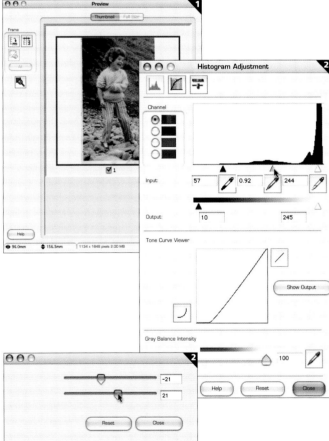

2 Having created a preview of the scan, you will usually have the option of adjusting the image before the final scan is made. In Epson's basic 'Home Mode', for example, you can adjust brightness and contrast levels, whereas if you are using the more sophisticated 'Professional Mode' you will have greater control over the scan.

3 Once you're happy with the preview view, click Scan to complete the scan. Depending on the resolution you've selected for your particular scan, the process will be complete within approximately 1–5 minutes.

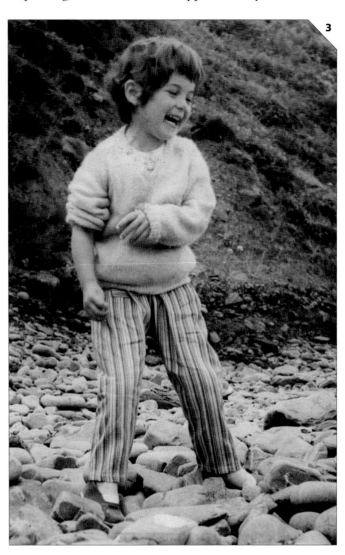

What resolution?

Deciding at what resolution to scan prints, negatives and transparencies can be confusing, as much will depend on how large the final image is intended to be used. Here are some useful guidelines:

Original Source	Use/Size	Scanning resolution
Print	Web	72–100ppi
Print	Same size as original	200–300ppi
Print	Twice size as original	400–600ppi
Print	Four times original	800–1,200ppi
Print	Half size of original	100–150ppi
35mm neg/slide	6 x 4in (15 x 10cm)	1,200ppi
35mm neg/slide	10 x 8in (25 x 20cm)	2,400ppi
35mm neg/slide	18 x 10in (46 x 25cm)	3,600ppi

Printers

Once you've captured your images, either via a camera or scanner, sooner or later you'll want to start printing your favourite images to show friends and relatives, or even to exhibit. Home printing, either direct from the camera or via a computer, is increasing in popularity and there is now a huge variety of printers available for the job.

Inkjet

The once-lowly inkjet printer was given a new lease of life with the advent of digital photography. At one point it seemed that the laser printer would supersede the inkjet, but it quickly transpired that inkjet technology lent itself perfectly to digital imaging and today, despite there being affordable colour laser and thermal (or dye sub) printers emerging onto the market, inkjet printers still provide the highest-quality images for the price.

Size

Inkjet printers are available in a wide variety of sizes. On the one hand, there are small 'portable' models that print standard 6 x 4in (15 x 10cm) prints, which are ideal for family holiday snaps, while at the other end of the scale, there are professional printers capable of producing poster-sized prints. If you're an enthusiastic amateur, it's certainly worth buying a printer capable of printing A4-size paper. It doesn't mean you can print only A4 – a tray will hold and feed smaller-sized paper for printing snaps – but it does give you the option of producing good-sized prints of your favourite images should you wish to display them framed and hung on a wall. You may even want to consider an A3 printer, bearing in mind that in the longer term the paper and inks will cost a lot more than the printer itself, which may not cost a great deal more than an A4 printer.

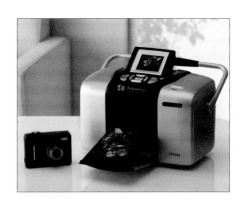

Dots per inch

A printer's ability to resolve fine detail, in other words its resolution, is measured in dots per inch (dpi), which should not to be confused with the image's own resolution, which is measured in pixels per inch (ppi). A dpi figure tells you how many droplets of ink the printer is capable of printing on an inch of paper, so the higher the number the greater the resolution. Most printers today have settings ranging from 360dpi, through to 720dpi, 1,440dpi and up to 2,880dpi. The lowest resolution should be used for basic print jobs such as letters, using standard plain paper, while the higher resolutions should be used in conjunction with higher grades of photographic-quality paper. The paper you buy should tell you what resolution can be used. Printing with a high-resolution setting on standard paper will simply result in too much ink being applied.

Numbers of colours

Another aspect to consider when assessing an inkjet is the number of different colours it uses. All inkjet printers use the basic secondary

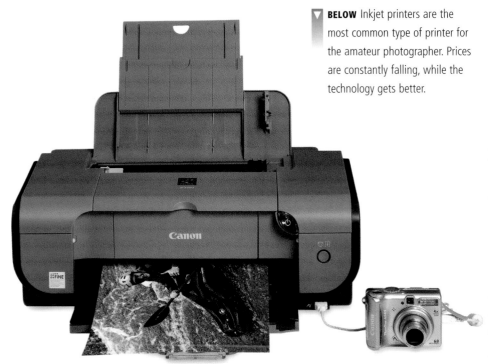

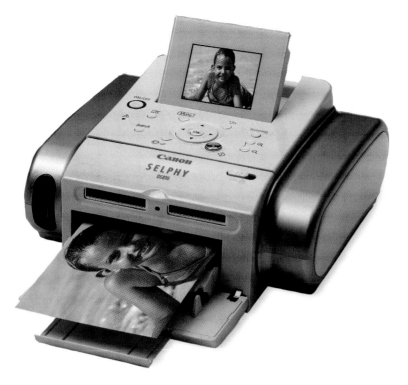

LEFT Dye-sublimation, or dye-sub printers, are mainly limited to 6 x 4in (15 x 10cm) print sizes, although some larger models are made. They tend to have a higher cost per print than inkjet printers.

colours – cyan, magenta and yellow (CMY) – to replicate the reds, greens and blues (RGB) of the digital image and, in addition, all printers also use a black ink (K) to add depth to darker regions of an image. While in theory, CMYK are the only colours you need to produce all the visible colours of the spectrum, some of the more sophisticated printers have additional colours, such as light cyan and light magenta, to improve subtle colour gradation. Some even include an additional light black or grey for improved neutral tones in black and white prints.

Direct to printer

You don't have to own a computer to enjoy the benefits of photographic-quality home printing. A number of manufacturers, such as Canon and Epson, produce printers that can print directly from a digital camera or a memory card. Such printers are capable of producing excellent results, but be certain to look into how much editing can be undertaken. Some, for example, will only allow simple cropping, while others may have the option of making brightness and tonal corrections and other more sophisticated adjustments. However

comprehensive the 'in-printer' editing capabilities, they will still pale into insignificance compared with what can be achieved using image-editing software.

Dye-sub printers

Although inkjets are the most popular photographic-quality printers for the home, there are alternatives. There is an increasing number of dye-sublimation printers available on the market. Most are small, portable printers producing 6 x 4in (15 x 10cm) prints, and many have been designed to print directly from a camera or memory card.

Dye-sub printers use cassette-like cartridges that are loaded with strips of cyan-, magenta- and yellow-coloured ribbon. An additional clear coating ribbon is used to add a protective coating to the prints. As the paper passes through the printer, the colour ribbon is heated and the dye in the ribbon transferred to the paper. The paper passes through the printer four times before

RIGHT An Epson Aculaser C1100. There was a time when it seemed that colour laser printers would be a popular choice for photographers, but inkjet and dye-sub technology took over.

the final, protected image is complete. If you're considering a dye-sub printer, don't be thrown by the advertised resolutions of 300 – 400dpi. Because dye-subs work in a different way to inkjets, these comparatively low resolution figures actually equate to a very high print resolution. In fact, dye-sub prints probably resemble traditional colour prints much more closely than inkjet prints in terms of feel and texture.

When it comes to image quality, many claim dye-sub printers to be as good as inkjets, but print for print they tend to be a little more expensive, particularly the less common A4-sized (letter) printers. However, with more and more people buying these small but sturdy printers, it's possible that the consumables will come down in price.

Laser printers

While affordable laser colour printers are now available, these still tend to be used in offices for producing large numbers of colour reports or similar uses. Laser printers are not yet as close to photographic-quality prints as inkjet and dye-sub printers and are rarely thought of for home use.

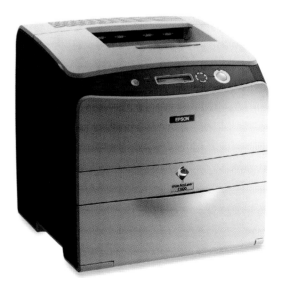

Paper and Ink

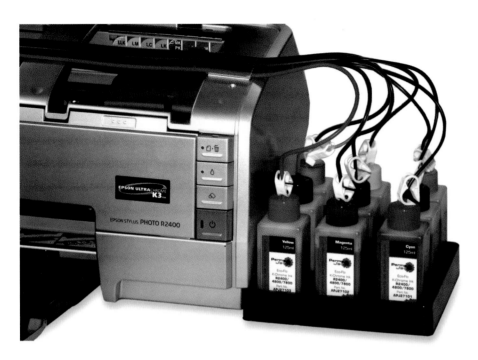

LEFT Inkflow systems like these mean you don't have to change your cartiridges as often. The cost per print tends to be cheaper with bulk systems, too.

No matter how much you pay for an inkjet printer, there are two further factors that will certainly govern the quality of the prints it produces – paper and ink. Using cheap, inferior consumables is likely to cost you far more in the long run.

Paper

To achieve the best-possible print quality from your printer, consider carefully the paper you're using. As a rule of thumb, the heavier the paper, the better it is likely to be. If you've ever tried printing a colour picture onto plain copy paper you'll know how dismal the results can be, as the inks spread and the colours appear dull and muted. Such paper weighs around 80gsm (grams per square metre). To achieve 'true' photographic-quality prints – be wary of the names manufacturers give to their various papers – you'll need to use a paper weighing between 210 to 250gsm. Unfortunately, compared with lighter papers, such heavyweight paper is quite expensive, particularly

in A4 or A3 (letter or tabloid) sizes. With such paper costing a premium, you may want to use a lightweight paper for proofing, and smaller sizes for your holiday and family snaps.

Inks

As well as paper weight and quality, the inks you use will also affect how good your prints look, and how long they last. There are numerous third-party ink manufacturers that on the surface provide much better value for money than the branded inks produced by companies such as Epson and Canon. But, although such inks are less expensive, it may well be the case that they are a false economy. First, third-party inks may not provide you with the quality you want for your prints, and, second, it's likely that they will fade much quicker, particularly if exposed to daylight.

RIGHT The paper you use for your prints will play a big part in print quality. For your best photographs, make prints on the best quality paper.

Of course, these inks have a use for producing short-lived 'fun' projects, such as greetings cards, or proofs, but if you want the best-possible quality and longest-lasting prints, the best solution is to use inks produced by the same manufacturer as the printer.

Ink flow

One alternative that may offer some savings, particularly for medium-to-heavy print usage, is an inkflow system. Offered by companies such as Lyson (www.lyson.com) and Permajet (www.permajet.com), these systems feature large refillable ink containers that are connected to the printer via a series of narrow tubes, which in turn connect to the printer nozzles.

Although initial start-up costs can be quite expensive, when it comes to refilling, the inks are much cheaper to buy separately compared with buying an entire set of colour cartridges.

In addition, the various coloured inks are used and replaced individually, so you only need to replace those colours that have run empty.

With some colour cartridges, you have to replace the whole cartridge as soon as one colour runs out. As well as the financial incentive an inkflow system may offer, there's also an environmental advantage that all of us should consider.

Specialist inks

Lyson and Permajet also manufacture specialist inks that are designed specifically for photographers using inkjet printers. As well as coloured inks, which are designed specifically for use in certain makes of printer, these companies also produce a series of grey and black inks, which are used together to produce high-quality black and white prints. The use of grey inks in addition to black helps to highlight the subtle tones of the black and white image to their very best advantage.

Both these companies make strong claims for the longevity of their pigment-based inks, with some calculated to last over a hundred years before they begin to fade.

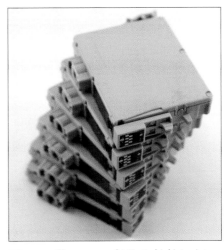

ABOVE The more sophisticated inkjet printers use individual colour cartridges, which means you only need to replace one at a time.

Leave it to the professionals

Although it's possible to achieve great-looking prints relatively easily in the comfort of your own home, it can take time, and many people simply do not get around to it. If this sounds all too familiar, it's worth considering one of the many on-line printing companies. You'll need a computer and Internet connection for this – and the faster the connection the better. A quick search on the web will throw up a number of companies. It's then simply a case of registering and following the instructions. This will involve uploading the images of which you want prints, making payment, and waiting for them to arrive by post (usually within a day or two). Buying a large number of prints this way is not only very easy, it can work out cheaper than printing them at home, and the results are usually excellent. Most on-line printing services offer more than just photographs. Photobooks, T-shirts, poster prints, mugs and greetings cards are just some of the more popular ways in which you can get your images into print. Most on-line companies also double up as on-line galleries where you can store and share your images.

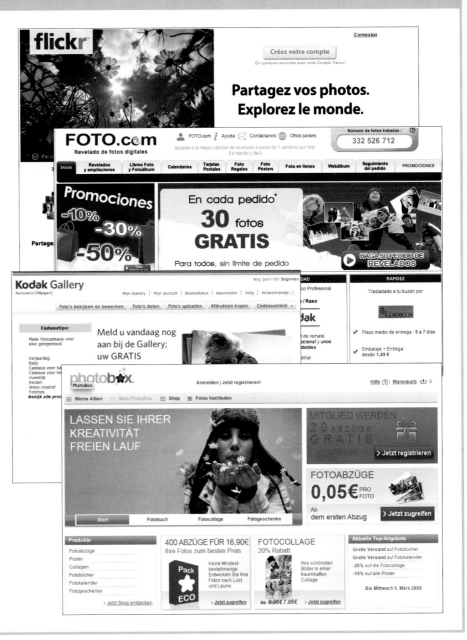

Printing

If you've only just bought a printer, you'll discover that it came with a CD. The disc will contain what's referred to as 'driver' software. This contains all the software needed for your computer to communicate with the printer. Without the driver software, the computer won't recognize the printer and you won't be able to print. To install the software, insert the disc into your computer's CD drive and follow the onscreen instructions. This should be very straightforward and take only a matter of minutes. If you've bought a used or refurbished printer and it doesn't have an accompanying CD, don't worry. Simply go on-line and search for the printer manufacturer. You'll find all the information you need on the website to download the driver software for your particular printer.

PRINTER OPTIONS AND FUNCTIONS

With the printer set up on your computer and running with good-quality inks and paper, photographic-quality prints are only a few clicks away. Printing is a straightforward process, but there are one or two things to look out for when you first start. Let's run through a typical print job using Photoshop Elements – other software will have very similar commands and dialog boxes.

1 Once you've completed editing an image in Edit mode and you're ready to print, go to File > Print. This will bring up the Print dialog window. Under the Printer's drop-down menu, select the name of your printer.

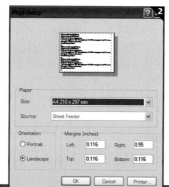

2 Make sure that your image is going to print in the correct format. In this example, a landscape-format image is incorrectly set up to print in portrait format. To correct this, click on the landscape/portrait format icons in the lower left-hand part of the dialog window.

Before you start printing, it's important to make sure that you have the correct paper size and type set up. Click on Page Setup in the lower right-hand corner of the dialog window.

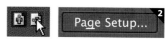

3 In the Page Setup dialog box, choose the paper size from the Size drop-down menu. Here, we've chosen A4.

Click on the Printer tab to bring up the printer's Properties window. There are a number of controls here, but the most important is the Media Type drop-down menu. Click on the type of paper on to which you're going to print. The menu attempts to cover the most common terms used by paper manufacturers.

Once you're happy with the settings, click OK to return to the Page Setup window. Here, click OK again to return to Element's Print dialog window.

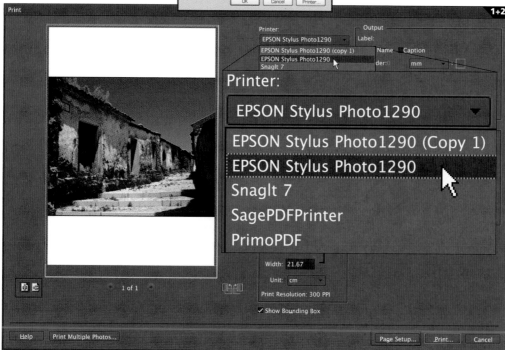

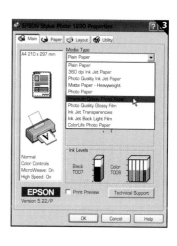

4 With the correct paper size and type selected, it's time to finalize how the image looks on the page before printing. Under the Print Size menu the image will default to Actual Size.

In a way this size is not important, and what's more relevant is checking to see what the Print Resolution figure is toward the bottom of the window, in the Scaled Print Size area. Here, the image is going to print at a healthy 300ppi, which is the optimum print setting. The outer edge of the white border in the preview window represents the size of the paper.

5 But note what happens to the Print Resolution figure if we scale the image down or up. Selecting a smaller print size ($3^1/2$ x 5in / 8.9 x 12.7cm) from the Print Size drop-down menu has seen the Print Resolution increase to 546ppi, while selecting a larger print size (8 x 10in / 20.3 x 25.4cm) results in the resolution falling to 255ppi. With the 'Show Bounding Box' checked, you can rescale the image by dragging one of the corner boxes.

If, when you first go to print your image, only a small part of it appears in the preview box, and it's entirely covering the preview paper area, check to see what the print resolution is. It may be that your camera saves files at 72ppi, which is not a problem, but it means you will have to rescale the image before printing. Check the Scale to Fit Media box and note the percentage reading. Uncheck the Scale to Fit Media box, input a smaller percentage than you noted, and you should then be able to see the corners of the Bounding Box to help you scale the image. Scale the image to the size you want it to appear on the page. Check the resolution is a satisfactory 200ppi or more, and then click Print.

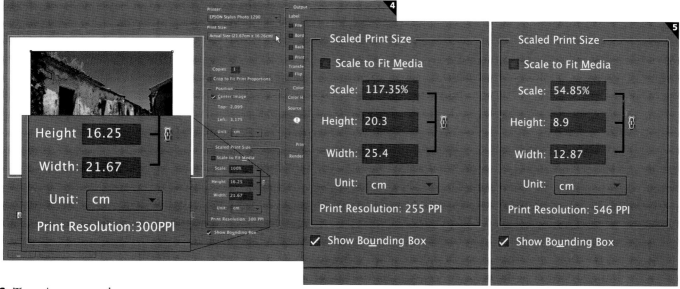

6 To print more than one image on a page, click the Print Multiple Images box in the Print dialog window. This will bring up a Print Photos window. In the Select Type of Print menu, you have various print styles, from Contact Sheet to Picture Package.

7 In the Select Layout menu, you can select how you want your image to appear and whether or not to add a preset border style. The window to the left allows you to add and delete images from the selection.

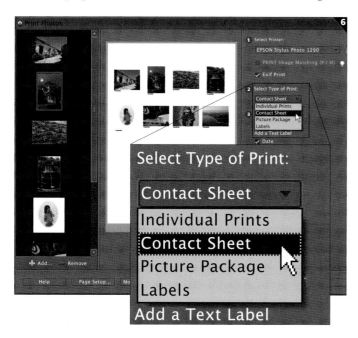

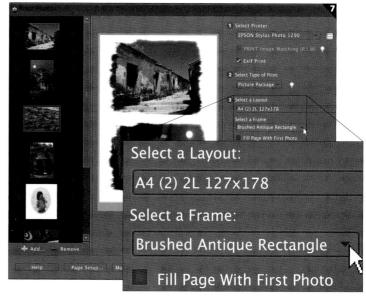

E-mailing Photographs

With so many people now connected to the World Wide Web, more and more of us are staying in touch with friends and family via e-mail. With broadband Internet access becoming increasingly widespread, it is now viable to send images without fear of wasting the recipient's time as they download relatively large files. Even so, unless you know that images are specifically going to be required for printing, it still pays to reduce file sizes for onscreen viewing. The more sophisticated image-editing software packages make it very simple to e-mail images.

SHARING YOUR IMAGES

1 Using Elements to send images via e-mail only takes a few clicks of the mouse. Select Share in the main viewing window and click the E-mail Attachments button to bring up the E-mail dialog window, where you can choose your preferred e-mail application.

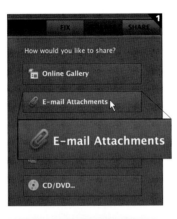

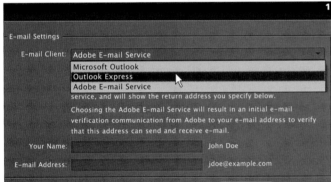

2 If the image you want to send is open in the Edit window, it will automatically be selected and placed in the E-mail Attachments window. In the same window, click the Convert Photos to JPEG box, as this is by far the most efficient format in which to e-mail images. Elements' default Maximum Photo Size settings are fairly standard, and images measuring 800 x 600 pixels will display well on most computers, including laptops. If you have

specific needs, then you can select smaller or bigger files. The Quality slider determines how much compression is applied to the image, and the lower the number, the greater the amount of compression that is applied. This will also lower the quality. The higher the number, the less compression is applied and the higher the quality.

Once you've chosen the image size and compression setting, Elements will tell you how large the file is and how long it estimates it will take to download via a slow, dial-up speed connection.

If you think the file is going to take too long to download, simply reduce the file size or increase the compression.

3 If you want to add any images, click the '+' symbol at the top of the E-mail Attachments window to bring up the Add Photos dialog window. From here you can navigate to your image collections and add whichever images you choose. When you've chosen, click Done to return to the E-mail Attachments window. If you're happy with your selection, click Next.

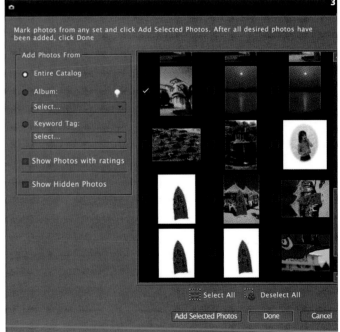

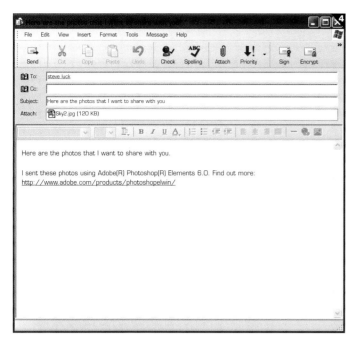

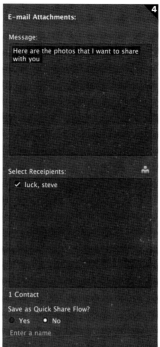

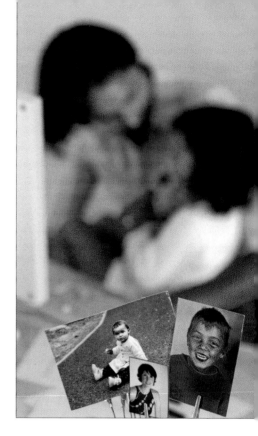

4 In the next screen you'll be given the option of typing your message and selecting the people to whom you want to send the images. After choosing the recipients, click Next and Elements will open up your preferred e-mail application with a pre-formatted new e-mail message to your list of recipients, containing your images and accompanying message. Now all you have to do is send.

▲ **ABOVE** Sharing images via email has never been so simple. Images can be sent aross the world in a matter of moments.

MANUAL RESIZING

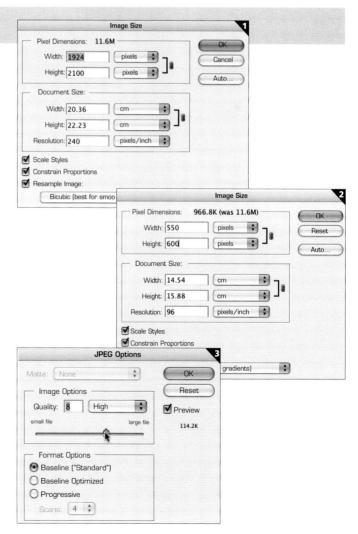

If you don't have Elements, and are unsure of how your software can automatically resize images, here's how to do it manually. All software can resize images in this way.

1 To resize an image for use on a website manually, go to Image > Resize > Image size. This brings up the Image Size dialog box. At nearly 12 MB the notional image is far too big to be used on the Internet.

2 Make sure the Resample Image box is ticked, and use Bicubic Sharper, as this is a specific algorithm for reducing image sizes. Change the image's resolution to 96ppi, which is the resolution for most Windows- based PC screens, and set the Height to

600 pixels, the optimum height for all screen images. This reduces the image's file size to 966K (just under 1MB), but this is still quite big for a web image.

3 Go to File > Save As and rename the file. Use a 'web' suffix so that you don't over-write the original, and select JPEG as the file format. Click OK, and the JPEG Options dialog window will appear. Here, a Quality compression setting of 8 has been chosen, which has reduced the file size to an acceptable 114 K.

You can also save the file as Progressive, which means that when it opens on screen, the image will appear quickly, but blurred, and gradually sharpen with the set number of scans selected.

Online Galleries

Photoshop Elements has a number of extremely useful automated tools to make editing images as easy as possible. One of the most useful is the Online Galleries command. Essentially, this allows you to select any number of your images; Elements will then resize them automatically, and place them in a pre-formatted gallery style. The gallery is then saved, ready for you to upload to the Internet, which is ideal for showing wedding or other special-event photographs to as many or as few people as you like, no matter where they live. If you have Photoshop, you can create similar galleries via the Browser window. Simply select the folder containing the images you want to use and then, still in the Browser window, go to Tools > Photoshop > Web Photo Gallery. There, you'll find a number of preset gallery styles to choose from. Once you've selected a gallery style, Photoshop will automatically resize the images and prepare the gallery for viewing in your web browser.

BUILDING AN ONLINE GALLERY

1 Before you start creating the Online Gallery, you may want to preselect the images you want to include in the Browser window. This will make the process quicker in the long run, but it's by no means essential. Nor do you need to resize any images manually to make them suitable for sending via e-mail – Elements will do this automatically.

To begin creating the gallery itself, click the Share tab to the top right of the Elements' window and then select Online Gallery.

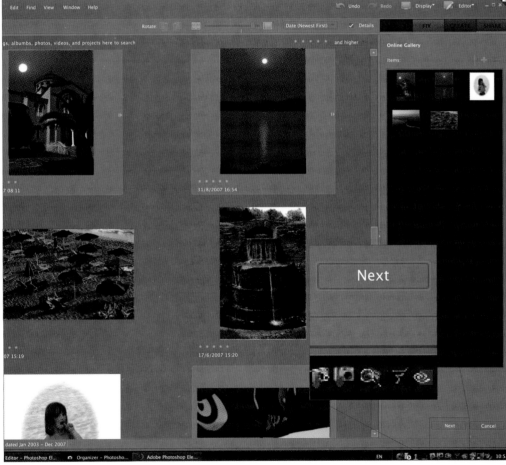

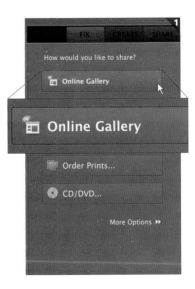

2 Click on the '+' symbol at the top of the first Online Gallery screen to navigate to the collection you made earlier. Drag the folder over to the window, or browse for individual images and drag them across one at a time. You can rearrange the order in which the images appear by dragging and placing the image thumb-nails in the small window. Once you've finalized your selection, click Next at the bottom of the window.

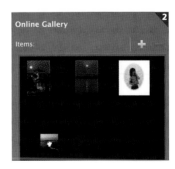

3 Elements will now present you with a variety of gallery templates to choose from. When you select a specific template, Elements provides a brief description of the

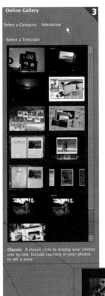

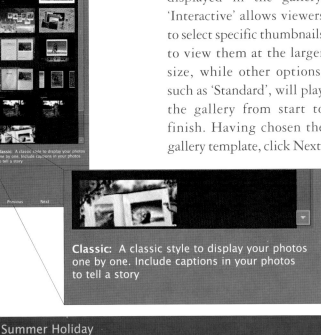

Classic: A classic style to display your photos one by one. Include captions in your photos to tell a story

template you've chosen at the bottom of the window, and also whether or not that template allows you to include captions. With such a diverse variety of gallery styles to choose from, you should easily find a style appropriate for your needs.

You can also choose how you want the images to be displayed in the gallery. 'Interactive' allows viewers to select specific thumbnails to view them at the larger size, while other options, such as 'Standard', will play the gallery from start to finish. Having chosen the gallery template, click Next.

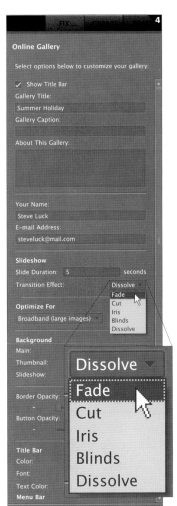

4 Depending on the chosen template, Elements will present you with a screen where you can customize your gallery. Here you can enter the gallery name and other details about the gallery, such as your name and e-mail address, so that people can easily see who the gallery is from and how to contact you.

In addition, and depending on the type of gallery, you can choose the transition effect (experiment to see which one you like best from the options given, such as Fade, Cut and so on). You can also choose how large you want the images to be saved. There are two standard settings – Broadband and Dial-up, which are self-explanatory. If you know that most of your viewers have a fast Internet connection, then select the first; otherwise it is safer to select the dial-up option.

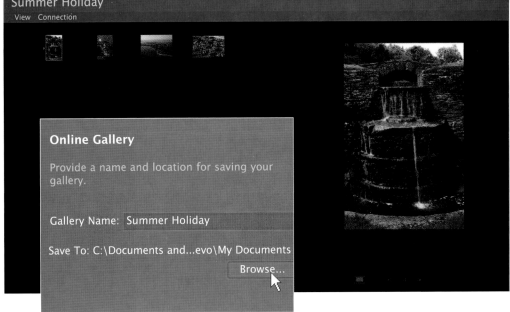

6 Finally, you have the option to upload and share your gallery using one of the options in the window. How you do this will depend on your Internet Service Provider (ISP). If you have any doubts on how do this, contact your ISP and they'll take you through the steps you need to take.

Elements also gives you the option of burning the gallery onto a CD should you wish to distribute it in this way.

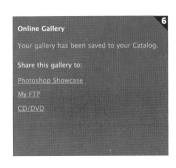

5 After a few minutes, Elements will present you with the complete gallery, which you can run to check that you're happy with it. If you want to change the

template style, go back to the Online Gallery window and select Previous, where you can then select another template. Alternatively, if you're happy with the

gallery, you will be asked to give it a name and choose a location to save it to on your hard drive. Once you've entered this information, click Next.

Slide Shows

Another excellent way to show off your pictures to friends and family is to create a slide show of your selected photographs – whether they're of a recent family holiday, a wedding or your new home. Most image-editing software packages offer this option, and Photoshop Elements is no exception. In a relatively short space of time you can use Elements' Slide Show option to create a professional-looking slide show featuring all your favourite images, accompanied by music, voiceovers and text, should you wish.

Perhaps somewhat surprisingly, this attractive feature isn't available to Photoshop users, who will have to content themselves with using the Web Photo Gallery feature explained in the last project.

CREATING A SLIDE SHOW

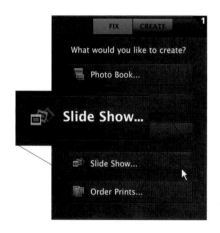

1 Before you start creating the show, you may want to place all the images you intend using in one easily identifiable folder. This will save time, but, as with the Online Gallery, it's not essential. To start, select the Slide Show option in the Create window.

2 The first window provides you with the basic options for the slide show. Most of the options are fairly self-explanatory, such as Static Duration, Transition Duration and Background Color. The Transition box provides a drop-down menu of the various transition styles available to you.

Although you may be tempted to use some of the more exotic-sounding styles, this can sometimes be a distraction, particularly if the Transition Duration is quite lengthy. You're better off keeping the transitions short and simple.

The Pan and Zoom option gives the slide show a professional feel, but it can be a bit too much if applied to all the slides – again, a case of less is more. If you don't click this option in the Slide Show Preferences window, you'll still have the option of applying Pan and Zoom transitions manually to the slides that you think are most suitable for the treatment. Once you've finished selecting your basic preferences, click OK.

3 Elements will now bring up the Slide Show Editor screen. Here, you can select the images you want to include in the slide show by clicking the Add Media button at the top of the screen. This will bring up the familiar Add Photos window, where you can navigate to the images you want to include. Once you've located the images, click Done at the bottom of the screen to return to the Slide Show Editor window.

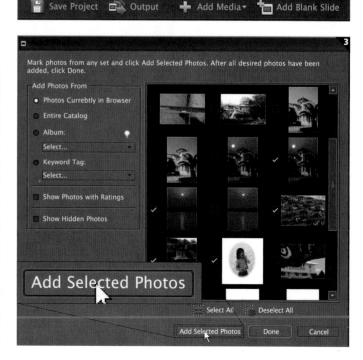

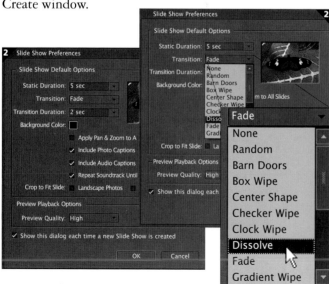

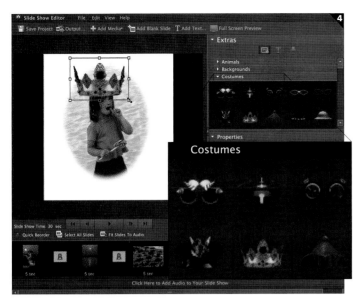

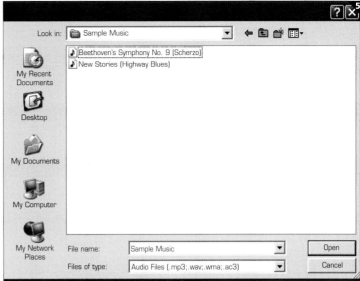

4 The Slide Show Editor is a powerful tool that enables you to customize all sorts of aspects of your show. The images you've selected will appear in a timeline at the bottom of the window. You can select individual images and apply a whole host of effects to them.

Many of the options are geared toward the fun side of slide shows, allowing you to add cartoon animals, different backgrounds, speech bubbles and costumes. If you're using the slide show to make a presentation, you can add text and narrative to make more serious points.

5 One of the most attractive aspects of Elements' slide shows is that it allows you to add sounds or music to your show. Selecting 'Click Here to Add Audio to Your Slide Show' near the bottom of the Editor window will bring up the 'Choose your Audio Files' dialog box.

From here, you can navigate to any music tracks that you might have stored on your computer, such as those you've downloaded for an MP3 player or those that were supplied when you purchased the software. Here, the Sample Music folder has been selected.

6 Once you have chosen your music, you'll see that the music appears as another line underneath your selection of images in the Editor window. You can edit the images to appear at specific points along the music timeline, which is useful if you've selected more than one piece of music. If you've only selected one track, the easiest option is to set the music to repeat and click the Fit Slides to Audio option.

Adding text is just as straightforward. Click the Add Text button and the Text Editor will appear. You can type in the text you want over any specific slide. You have the option of resizing and placing the text where you wish, and you can also change the font and colour of the text.

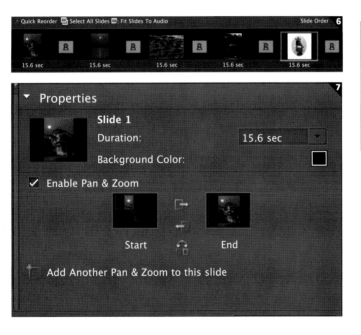

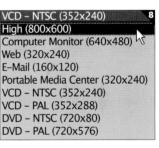

7 In the Properties window you can add a Pan and Zoom effect to individual slides. Click on Start and draw a green square around the area that you want to appear first when the image opens. Click on End and select the area that will complete the slide.

Here, for example, the slide will open with a close-up of the sun and pan out to reveal the entire image. To change the order of any of the images, simply click and drag. To preview the show, click Full Screen Preview at the top of the window.

8 When you're happy with the slide show, click Save Project in the top left corner of the Editor window and Elements will offer several ways to save the show – either as a file on your hard drive, on CD/DVD or straight to your television. Elements provides easy-to-follow instructions and advice to help you make the right choices for your show. A lot depends on how instantly you want to view the show and whether or not your prospective audience lives in the same home as you or on the other side of the world.

Index

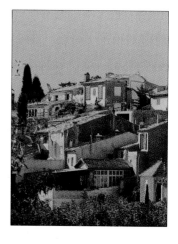

Acknowledgements

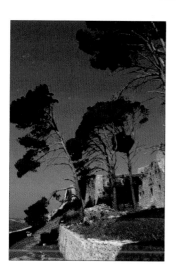

The publisher would like to thank the following for supplying photographs for this book: Canon UK Ltd 84 (b), 85 (t); Corbis 91 (tr); Dell Inc 8; Digital Vision 80 (l); Epson (UK) Ltd 82 (t), 84 (tr), 85 (br), 86 (t); ImageDJ 32 (c); iStock photography 86 (br), 87 (tr); LaCie Ltd 9; Photodisk 33 (l), 81 (c, r); Plustek Inc 82 (b).
All other images by Steve Luck.
Images are listed in clockwise order from the top (t = top, c = centre, b = bottom, r = right, l = left, tr = top right etc).

Every effort has been made to obtain permission to reproduce copyright material, but there may be cases where we have been unable to trace a copyright holder. The publisher will be happy to correct any omissions in future editions of this book.